# CAN I TRUST THE BIBLE?

# CAN I TRUST THE BIBLE?

*Important Questions Often Asked About the Bible . . . With Some Answers by Eight Evangelical Scholars*

*Edited by*
HOWARD F. VOS

MOODY PRESS
CHICAGO

# CONTENTS

*Chapter 1*

# HOW MAY I KNOW THE BIBLE IS INSPIRED?

*by*

GORDON H. CLARK

# Chapter 1

## HOW MAY I KNOW THE BIBLE
## IS INSPIRED?

THE QUESTION of this chapter concerns the inspiration of the Bible. It must be clearly distinguished from another question with which it might be confused: How may I know that the Bible is true? These two questions are indeed related, but they are not the same question. They have even been answered in opposite ways. The contemporary movement in theology called Neo-orthodoxy claims that the Bible is inspired, but also asserts that it is not completely true. And obviously some other book, such as Churchill's *The Gathering Storm*, could possibly be entirely true without being inspired. Such a book might even be called infallible. Truth and inspiration therefore must be distinguished.

The two ideas, however, are closely related, especially in the case of the Bible. The Neo-orthodox writers can hold to an inspired but mistaken Bible only because they have changed the meaning of inspiration. When the Biblical definition of inspiration is used, there can be no inspiration without truth, even though there often is truth without inspiration. For the Christian, therefore, the question of truth is a prior question, and unless the Bible is true, there is not much use in discussing inspiration.

Some of the evidence that the Bible is true is presented in other chapters of this book. Archaeological and historical research has corroborated Biblical history in numerous instances. This material will here be assumed.

9

In addition to historical evidence of the truth of the Bible, there must also be some logical support for the conclusion. If the Bible makes contradictory statements, then, regardless of archaeology and history, part of the Bible must be false. We may not know which half of the contradiction is false and which is true, but we would be logically certain that both parts cannot be true.

It is not the purpose of this chapter to discuss in detail any of the alleged contradictions. Most of them are based on rather transparent misinterpretations. A few remain as puzzles because we do not know enough about ancient conditions. Though we may guess how they can be explained, we have no objective evidence that our guesses are correct. However, to convict the Bible of inconsistency, there should be (1) several, (2) clear, and (3) important instances. But the unsolved instances are not many, and they are either unclear or unimportant. We are at liberty therefore to guess that they will not ultimately prove insoluble.

Now, then, is the Bible inspired? Its truth, or at least its general trustworthiness, is assumed; but we want to know whether the Bible like Churchill's *The Gathering Storm* is simply a history book that happens to be true, or whether it is the Word of God.

### The Biblical Claims

The first reason for believing the Bible is inspired is that the Bible claims to be inspired. When this reason is offered to an unbeliever, almost always his immediate reaction is derision. To him it is very much like putting a liar on the witness stand and having him swear to tell the truth. But why a liar? Do not honest witnesses also swear to tell the truth? Yet even a Christian with a smattering of logic may object to this procedure because it seems to beg the question. It is circular. We believe the Bible to be inspired because it makes the claim, and we believe the claim because it is inspired and therefore true. This does not seem to be the right way to argue.

It must be granted that not every claim is *ipso facto* true. There have been false witnesses in court, there have been false Messiahs, and there have been fraudulent so-called revelations. But to ignore the claim of the Bible, or of witnesses generally, is both an oversimplification and a mistake. For example, suppose the Bible actually says that it is not inspired. Or suppose merely that the Bible is completely silent on the subject, that it makes no more claim to divine inspiration than did Churchill. In such a case, if the Christian asserts that the book is inspired, the unbeliever would be sure to reply that he is going far beyond the evidence.

This reply is certainly just. There is no reason for making assertions beyond those that can be validly inferred from the statements of the Bible. But because this reply is so just, it follows that the unbeliever's derision at our first remark was groundless. What the Bible claims is an essential part of the argument. The Christian is well within the boundaries of logic to insist that the first reason for believing in the inspiration of the Bible is that it makes this claim.

The truth of a conclusion depends on the truth of its premises. This means that the next step is to show that as a matter of fact the Bible makes this claim. A good many people who have a fair knowledge of the contents of the Bible would be inclined to omit this step as unnecessary. Of course the Bible makes this claim. However, not everybody is so familiar with what the Bible says. Even those who have a fair knowledge may not realize how insistently the Bible makes this claim. And there are others who, troubled by critical problems and alleged inaccuracies, and yet desirous of retaining the Bible as very important or even as a necessary religious document, think that they can discard inspiration while retaining the Bible as a fairly reliable source of religious knowledge. Such people may think that there are just a few minor errors in the Bible or many errors or—as is particularly the case in this mid-twentieth century period—that the Bible is entirely fable. Nonetheless they hold to it as in some sense a religious guide. This very widespread view loses all semblance of logic when confronted with the actual claims to inspiration that we find throughout the whole Bible.

## THE MEANING OF INSPIRATION

There is another reason for canvassing the Biblical claims to inspiration. By doing so we shall come to see what the Bible means by inspiration. In recent theology the Bible has been called inspired in the sense that Shakespeare's plays may be called inspired. That is, they are inspiring; they excite us, they elevate our ideas, they enlarge our views and give us an understanding of human nature. On this meaning of inspiration it is usually said that not all parts of the Bible are equally inspired. The genealogies are dull and uninspiring.

But is this what the Bible means by inspiration? We should certainly be very careful to know what we mean when we discuss a subject. If two people have two different meanings in mind, their conversation will be at cross purposes and the one cannot understand the other. Similarly, if a person by himself studies inspiration, or any other subject, yet does not have a clear concept of what he is studying, he may not confuse anyone else so long as he keeps his thought to himself; but his thoughts in his own mind will be muddled and he will lack understanding. Unfortunately this is very often the case.

Perhaps the Bible's best known claim to inspiration is II Timothy 3:16: "All scripture is given by inspiration of God, and is profitable for doctrine," and so on. The English word *inspiration* with its prefix *in* gives the impression that after the Bible, or a book of the Bible, had been written, God breathed into it. However, the Greek word does not mean *breathed into,* it means *breathed out.* God breathed out the Scriptures. We might say metaphorically that the Scriptures are God's breath. Thus the claim is actually stronger than it appears in English.

### 1. *Plenary Inspiration*

Also to be noticed is the reference to *all* the Scripture. This idea we shall call the *plenary* inspiration of Scripture. God breathed out all of it. Differences in translation do not affect this point. The American Standard Version, Weymouth, and the German Bible have "every scripture"; the French translation, the Revised Standard Version, and Moffatt agree with the King James. It is a clear claim to plenary inspiration. To this verse may be added John 10:35, "the scripture cannot be broken." The precise point of Christ's remark is that all the Scripture is authoritative.

Another passage that bears examination is II Peter 1:20, 21: "No prophecy of the scripture is of any private interpretation. For the prophecy came not in old time by the will of man: but holy men of God spake as they were moved by the Holy Ghost." One might at first wonder whether there is some "scripture" that is not "prophecy," in which case this verse would not apply to all the Bible; it would apply only to the prophecies in the Bible and not to the rest of Scripture. A partial answer is that Moses was a prophet and that therefore even the book of Leviticus can be called prophecy. Prophecy is not necessarily prediction; it is any message from God. The phrase "prophecy of the scripture" simply means the divine message as written. Note next the universal negative: the verse says, "no prophecy." This covers it all.

Another difficulty is the word *private.* The contrast intended, however, is not with a supposed public interpretation, but with a *divine* interpretation. That is why verse 21 explains verse 20; otherwise the second verse would not be an intelligible reason for the first. No prophecy is of any private interpretation *because* prophecy (without exception; omit the article *the*) was never at any time brought by the will of man, but men spoke from God, being borne along by the Holy Ghost. Thus the passage is a strong assertion of the divine origin of the message.

Since the last reference raised the question whether all Scripture is prophecy, a few more verses relative to Moses may be added here. The main point, however, is not to show that Moses was a prophet, but rather to show the Bible's claim of inspiration. Of course Moses was a prophet: "This is that Moses, which said unto the children of Israel, A prophet shall the Lord your God raise up unto you of your brethren, like unto me; him shall ye hear" (Acts 7:37). "And there arose not a prophet since in Israel like unto Moses, whom the Lord knew face to face" (Deut. 34:10). This last verse indicates that Joshua was inferior to Moses, so that Moses could be compared only with Christ. Christ Himself said: "Had ye believed Moses, ye would have believed me: for he wrote of me. But if ye believe not his writings, how shall ye believe my words?" (John 5:46, 47).

That the prophetic authority mentioned in II Peter 1:21 applies to the entire Old Testament is shown not only in John 10:35, previously quoted, but also in many other passages. Romans 3:2 designates the entire Old Testament as the oracles of God. In Luke 24:44 Jesus places the Law of Moses, the Prophets, and the Psalms on the same level. Similar all-inclusive designations are found in Luke 24:25, 27; Matthew 5:17; 7:12; 11:13; Acts 3:21, 22; 26:22, 27; 28:23; Romans 3:21. Since these and other verses gather together the whole Old Testament into a unit, it becomes possible to extend to all whatever authority is asserted of any part.

Some very interesting claims are made of various parts. Peter in Acts 2:30 calls David a prophet, and David himself says, "The Spirit of the Lord spake by me, and his word was in my tongue" (II Sam. 23:2). Christ also (Mark 12:36) said that David spoke by the Holy Ghost. Quoting the second Psalm, Acts 4:25 asserts that the Lord spoke by David's mouth. This is not true of David alone, as was just explained, but God "spake by the mouth of his holy prophets, which have been since the world began" (Luke 1:70).

No doubt a few specific references to the later prophets should be added. Simple phrases, such as "the word of the Lord came unto me," and "the Lord said unto me," and "thus saith the Lord," are too numerous to list. They imply that it was the Lord who spoke through the mouth of the prophet (cf. Matt. 1:22; 2:15; Acts 3:18). There are, however, several instances where this idea is explicitly stated. "The Lord put forth his hand, and touched my mouth. And the Lord said unto me, Behold, I have put my words in thy mouth" (Jer. 1:9; cf. 9:12; 13:15; 30:4; 50:1). The same idea is expressed in Ezekiel 3:1, 4, 11, both pictorially and literally. After commanding Ezekiel to eat a scroll that was written within and without, the Lord tells him to "speak with my words unto them."

Such are the claims made by and for the Old Testament. But the Old Testament looks forward to a further and fuller revelation, one in which the Old Testament prophecies find their culmination, and which, therefore, if not superior in authorship, is certainly not inferior. If the inspiration of the Old Testament can be defended, the case for the New Testament should be granted without further argument. However, for greater completeness, something will be said about the New Testament claims for itself.

As the material is extensive, only a few passages are selected for comment. Jesus (Matt. 11:9-15) asserted that John the Baptist was a prophet and more than a prophet. He was superior to all the Old Testament prophets. Yet the prophet who was least in New Testament times was a greater prophet

than John. It follows, does it not, that the New Testament
prophets were no less inspired than their forerunners.

Romans 16:25-27 and Ephesians 3:4, 5 are similar. The
first passage speaks of a mystery that was not revealed in
the Old Testament but is now published in the writings of
the New Testament prophets. In the second passage Paul
claims for himself and the other apostles and prophets a
fuller knowledge than that revealed in earlier ages. ∗

Next, I Corinthians 12:28, in listing the ranks of office
in the church, places apostles above prophets. Ephesians
4:11 does the same thing. Therefore these verses as clearly
as the previous passages imply that the New Testament is no
less authoritative than the Old.

In I Corinthians 14:37 Paul says: "If any man think himself
to be a prophet, or spiritual, let him acknowledge that the
things that I write unto you are the commandments of the
Lord." This bears essentially the same meaning as Jeremiah's
claim that God put His own words into Jeremiah's mouth.

A further idea is found in Colossians 4:16. Here Paul
commands the reading of his letters in the churches. Just
as Isaiah or Jeremiah was to be read in the synagogues, so
by apostolic command the epistles were made a part of
the worship of the church. If someone objects that this
applies only to the the letters and to the churches of Colosse
and Laodicea, I, Thessalonians 5:27 extends the idea. Here
too we have an example of the apostolic imposition of the
New Testament Scriptures.

There are many pertinent passages, but II Peter 3:15, 16
will be used as a final example. In this place Peter is speaking of the Pauline epistles. "Even as our beloved brother
Paul also according to the wisdom given unto him hath written unto you; as also in all his epistles, speaking in them
of these things . . . which they that are unlearned and un-
stable wrest, as they do also the other scriptures, unto their
own destruction." From the way in which Peter speaks of

all Paul's epistles, it would seem that they are considered as a section of the New Testament canon, just as one might speak of the major prophets. Peter clearly regards them as a unit. Furthermore, he classifies them with "the other scriptures"; that is, he places them at least on a level with the Old Testament. And since in verse 2 of the same chapter Peter ranks himself and the other apostles with the holy prophets, it may be validly inferred that the Bible as a whole, both Old and New Testaments, claims to have been breathed out by God so that it cannot be broken.

Before we advance from the Biblical claims to the next stage of the argument, the significance of the passages quoted still needs some further elucidation. It has already been shown that the Bible teaches plenary inspiration. Plenary inspiration means that the Bible is inspired in all its parts. There is no section of it that was not breathed out by God. Nehemiah 7, with all its names and numbers, is just as much inspired as John 14.

### 2. *Verbal Inspiration*

In the next place, the Bible teaches verbal inspiration. God put words into Jeremiah's mouth. Possibly Jeremiah or some other prophet failed to grasp the thought, as I Peter 1:11 indicates; but the words were God's words. This is what is meant by verbal inspiration.

Unfortunately, verbal inspiration has been caricatured by its enemies, and the teaching of historic Protestantism has been misrepresented. Since therefore we wish to be clear in our own minds as well as to expose the blunders of unbelievers, a digression is called for.

The opponents falsely claim that verbal inspiration is a theory of mechanical dictation. They suppose that when God in Deuteronomy 18:18 says, "I will put my words in his mouth," the prophet is to be regarded as a sort of dictaphone, or at best as a stenographer whose personality is only minimally engaged in the transaction. This is obviously not true, because Jeremiah's style is not Isaiah's and Paul does not write like John. Neither Luther nor Calvin, nor recent orthodox theologians like Warfield, ever held a theory of mechanical dictation. It is a caricature invented by unbelievers.

At the same time it is incumbent on the believer to explain how God could put His own words into the mouth of a prophet without reducing him to the level of a disinterested stenographer. This is not at all difficult. The slightest understanding of the relation between God and a prophet leads one quickly away from the idea of modern office procedure.

When God wished to make a revelation, at the time of the exodus or of the captivity, He did not suddenly look around, as if caught unprepared, and wonder what man he could use. We cannot suppose that He advertised for a stenographer, and, when Moses and Jeremiah applied for the position, that God dictated His message. The relation between God and a prophet was not like that at all. A boss must take what he can get; he depends on the high school or business college to have taught the applicant shorthand and typing. But if we consider the omnipotence and wisdom of God, a very different picture emerges. God is the Creator. He made Moses. And when God wanted Moses to speak for Him, He said, "Who hath made man's mouth? Have not I, the Lord?"

Put it this way: God, who worketh all things according to His will and who hath done whatsoever He pleased, for no one can stay His hand or say, what doest Thou, from all eternity decreed to lead the Jews out of slavery by the hand of Moses. To this end He so controlled events that Moses was born at a given date, placed in the water to save him from an early death, found by Pharaoh's daughter, given the best Egyptian education possible, driven into the wilderness to learn patience, and in every detail so prepared by heredity and environment that when the time came, Moses' mentality and literary style were instruments precisely fitted to speak God's words. Between Moses and God there was an inner union, an identity of purpose, a co-operation of will, such that the words Moses wrote were God's own words and Moses' own words at the same time.

This has been a slight digression for the purpose of exposing a liberal misrepresentation of verbal inspiration and of thus further clarifying the Christian position. It is now time to return to the main line of the argument. Plenary inspiration has been defined; verbal inspiration has now been explained; one further point remains to be made concerning the Bible's claims for itself.

## A WRITTEN REVELATION

The Biblical revelation, the message that was breathed out by God, is a written revelation. The idea is not, or at least not merely, that the *prophets* were inspired. It is true of course that they were borne along by the Holy Ghost; but the Biblical claim is that God inspired what was *written*. In II Timothy 3:16 the writers are not even mentioned. Nor is it the full truth that the public speaking of the prophets and apostles was inspired. It is the *Scriptures*, the writings, that cannot be broken. The doctrine of plenary and verbal inspiration attaches first of all to the written word.

Toward the end of the nineteenth century a phrase came into use for the purpose of minimizing and in fact denying plenary inspiration. The modernists often said that the Bible contains the Word of God. Of course in one sense this is true. The Bible contains the Gospel of John, for example, and this Gospel or at least chapter 14 is God's Word. Thus the Bible contains the Word of God. But this is not what the modernists meant. They meant that some of the Bible is not God's Word. And because the phrase was true in one sense, it served as a diplomatic disguise for modernistic intention. Few Bible believers are any longer deceived by this language. They know that "the Bible contains the Word of God" is intended as a denial that "the Bible is the Word of God."

But now, in the middle of the twentieth century, modernism has become somewhat antiquated, and Neo-orthodoxy has taken its place. This movement has invented a new deceptive phrase. The Neo-orthodox people say that the Bible is a *record* of God's revelation. This phrase is also true in a sense. God revealed Himself to Moses and to Jeremiah, and the Bible is the record of those events. This true sense, however, is a deceptive disguise to cover a repudiation of the Biblical position. The Neo-orthodox writers as well as the modernists intend to deny that the Bible is the Word of God. Moses and Jeremiah may have received revelations, these writers say, but these revelations may have consisted only of historical events, or possibly of subjective emotions, but not of words. Thus the Bible becomes a record of Moses' experience rather than a verbally inspired message.

At the present time many people are still deceived by this Neo-orthodox phrase. No doubt in the future, recognition of its anti-Biblical meaning will become common. In the meantime attention must be patiently called to all the passages quoted above. They show that the Bible does not regard itself as a mere record of a past revelation. It is the revelation itself. It is itself the Word of God. It is the written words that God inspired. It is the Writings that cannot be broken.

The argument so far has shown that the Bible claims to be inspired, and in so doing has explained what inspiration is. If the reader already accepts the Bible as the Word of God, the question that forms the title of this chapter, "How May I Know the Bible Is Inspired?" has been answered. But perhaps the "I" in the title, a reader of this chapter, does not accept the Bible as the Word of God. Such a person will say, "No doubt the Bible claims inspiration, but is the claim true?" The question then becomes, How may one prove Biblical inspiration to an inquirer?

## *The Proof of Inspiration*

The point has already been made that to convince a person of the Bible's inspiration it is proper and virtually indispensable to show that the Bible claims inspiration. If the Bible made no such claim, it would be very difficult to defend the doctrine of inspiration. Now, although not every claim is true, for some persons and some books make false claims, the manner in which the Bible claims to be inspired limits us to a very narrow range of choice. Only a minor fraction of the claims has been explicitly quoted in this chapter. If all the Biblical references to its own inspiration were quoted, it would be clear that this claim is thoroughly pervasive. It cannot be regarded as an accidental blunder in one or two books, nor as an excess of temporary enthusiasm in one or two writers. The claim to inspiration pervades the Bible throughout.

If Moses and the prophets were mistaken in making this claim, if the apostles likewise were deceived, and if our Lord Himself entertained wrong notions of verbal inspiration, what assurance may anyone have relative to other matters about which they wrote? Is there any reason to suppose that men who were so uniformly in error as to the source of their message could have had any superior insight and accurate knowledge of man's relation to God? Why should we today believe that God so loved the world or that a sinner is justified by faith, if it was not God who gave John and Paul this information? And finally, who can profess a personal attachment to Jesus Christ and yet consistently contradict His assertion that the Scriptures cannot be broken? Therefore one is limited to a very narrow choice. Either the Bible is a worthless fraud and Jesus was a deluded martyr, or the Bible is in truth the Word of God written.

When people see that they are shut up to these two choices, some of them, because they cannot deny the general trustworthiness of the Bible as evidenced by archaeology and because they feel compelled to acknowledge its spiritual excellence, will be induced to accept plenary and verbal inspiration. Others, however, will choose the opposite. Recognizing more clearly that the teachings of the Bible form a seamless garment, they will in consistency reject the Bible *in toto,* repudiate its ideals, and look with pity or scorn on its deluded Messiah.

If a believer wishes to defend the claims of Christianity in the face of such a consistent rejection, and of course the believer is under obligation to do so, he must first of all consider the nature of proof and argument. It would be a blunder to rely on an invalid argument. It is poor strategy to underestimate the strength of the enemy. We ought to know precisely what proves what. We must know the necessary conditions of a valid argument. On what premises can the conclusion be based? And if we have found a satisfactory premise, how can we get the unbeliever to accept it? All this is part of the general defense of Christianity, known as apologetics. But as general apologetics is very extensive, the present discussion will be limited, so far as possible, to inspiration.

Almost a century ago Francis L. Patton, prominent for fifty years in the cause of conservative Christianity, defended inspiration by an argument of four steps. First, historical criticism shows that the history of the Bible is generally correct. Second, we then discover from the style, the information, and the harmony of the parts that they were written by a supernatural agency. Third, we note that the writers claimed inspiration. Therefore, fourth, we infer that the Bible is infallibly inspired. Patton supported point two as follows: "We know that the doctrines of the Bible have God's sanction. For what is Hebrew history but a long lesson in monotheism? . . . What was the sacrificial system but a divine exposition of the doctrine of guilt? . . . Their inherent excellence witnesses to their heavenly origin."

Today such an argument sounds naive. Patton's essential point is weak and his support is weaker. His view of Hebrew history, of its monotheism, of the purpose of the sacrificial system, as well as the style and the inherent excellence, are not premises an unbeliever will accept. People today simply do not believe that the sacrificial system is a divine exposition of guilt—and they may think that guilt is a sign of mental illness—nor do they agree that Biblical doctrine is inherently excellent.

The harmony of the parts is a more valuable point. For although the unbeliever asserts that there are innumerable inconsistencies throughout the Bible, patient exposition might convince him that its teaching is more consistent than he thinks. But the modern public have an ingrained belief that the Bible is self-contradictory, and it is extremely difficult to convince them otherwise. Yet, for reasons that will become clearer as we proceed, the attempt to show the Bible's logical consistency is, I believe, the best method of defending inspiration. But because it is so intricate and difficult, one naturally wonders about an easier method.

Here again we must consider the nature and limits of "proof." Demonstrative proof, such as occurs in geometry, depends on unproved axioms. However valid the demonstration may be, if two people do not accept the same axioms, they will not be convinced by the same proof. Is there then any proposition which the believer and the unbeliever will both accept without proof?

In times past there have been areas of agreement. Non-Christians would admit that God exists. During the Reformation the truthfulness of the Scripture was so widely taken for granted that the evidences seemed to furnish conclusive proof to any normal mind. But this situation no longer exists. Not only do most people reject the truthfulness of the Bible, but many also reject belief in God. Luther and Calvin did not have to face instrumentalism and logical positivism. Today these two philosophies are widely influential. In times past it was generally agreed that Jesus' moral standards were admirable. But today His ideas on marriage and labor problems are rejected even by some so-called Christian churches, and the rest of His morality is said to be inadequate at best.

The more consistent unbelief is, the less can agreement be obtained. So long as the unbeliever is inconsistent, we can force him to make a choice. If he inconsistently admires Jesus Christ or values the Bible, while at the same time he denies plenary and verbal inspiration, we can by logic insist that he accept both—or neither. But we cannot by logic prevent him from choosing neither and denying a common premise. It follows that in logical theory there is no proposition on which a consistent believer and a consistent unbeliever can agree. Therefore the doctrine of inspiration, like every other Christian doctrine, cannot be demonstrated to the satisfaction of a clear thinking unbeliever.

If, nonetheless, it can be shown that the Bible, in spite of having been written by more than thirty-five authors over a period of fifteen hundred years, is logically consistent, then the unbeliever would have to regard it as a most remarkable accident. It seems more likely that a single superintending mind could produce this result than that it just happened accidentally. Logical consistency therefore is evidence of inspiration; but it is not demonstration. Strange accidents do indeed occur, and no proof is forthcoming that the Bible is not such an accident. Unlikely perhaps, but still possible.

How then may an unbeliever be brought to admit the inspiration of the Scripture? Or, for it is the same question, how did "I" come to accept inspiration?

## The Testimony of the Holy Spirit

At the time of the Reformation when Luther and Calvin appealed to the Scriptures, the Roman Church argued that it and it alone accredited the Scriptures, and that therefore the Protestants could not legitimately use the Scriptures without first submitting to Rome. People were supposed to accept God's Word only on the authority of the church.

Against this claim the reformers developed the doctrine of the testimony of the Holy Spirit. The belief that the Bible is the Word of God, so they taught, is neither the result of a papal pronouncement, nor a conclusion inferred from prior premises; it is a belief which the Holy Ghost Himself produces in our minds. Calvin wrote: "It is therefore such a persuasion as requires no reason; such a knowledge as is supported by the highest reason and in which the mind rests with greater security and constancy than in any reasons; in fine, such a sense as cannot be produced but by a revelation from heaven" (*Institutes*, I, vii, 5).

Today this doctrine is easily misunderstood. Twentieth century Protestantism is largely infected with unbelief— much of it is scarcely Christian at all. Many small groups that profess loyalty to God's Word have lost, forgotten, or discarded whole sections of the rich theology of the sixteenth and early seventeenth centuries. They teach a diluted and impoverished Christianity. And underlying both these factors is the essential secularism and paganism of our civilization. Therefore the idea of the testimony of the Holy Spirit, if known at all, is subject to misunderstanding. Let us then try to spell it out in simple terms.

The first phrase in the quotation from Calvin includes and goes beyond what has already been emphasized. Reasons or premises by which to prove the authority of Scripture cannot be used because the consistent unbeliever will not accept any Christian premise. In addition, even a Christian in his own thought cannot construct a formal demonstration of the authority of Scriptures because all Christian syllogisms are grounded on that authority. We can believe the doctrine of the atonement only on the authority of Scripture, but we cannot believe the Bible on the authority of the atonement.

The second phrase in the quotation from Calvin says that the mind can rest in this knowledge with greater security than in any reasons. This is obvious because the security of a conclusion can be no greater than that of the premise on which it is based. That the sum of the squares on the other two sides is equal to the square of the hypotenuse cannot be any more certain than the axioms from which it is deduced.

But the third phrase of the quotation comes to the most important point. All along the problem has been how to accept a premise. Conclusions follow automatically; but what makes a man accept an initial proposition? Calvin's answer is plain: belief in the Scripture "cannot be produced but by a revelation from heaven." And on this most important point the possibility of misunderstanding is greatest.

What is a revelation from Heaven? It could be a message delivered by angels, such as Abraham received. It could be the finger of God writing on tablets of stone or on the wall of a palace. It could be a vision, such as John had on Patmos. And such things, unfortunately, are what most people think of when they hear of the testimony of the Spirit. Unwise Christian workers, careless of their language, sometimes describe their experience in glowing terms and embroider it beyond reality. When younger Christians do not see such visions or dream such dreams, they suffer disillusionment.

But there are other forms of revelation. Jesus once asked, "But whom say ye that I am?" And Peter replied, "Thou art the Christ." Then Jesus said, "Flesh and blood hath not re-

vealed it unto thee, but my Father which is in heaven" (Matt.
16:15-17). Peter had had neither trance nor vision, nor had
he heard an audible voice. In modern American slang we
would say, it just "dawned" on him. What happened was
that the Spirit produced this conviction in Peter's mind. I
should judge that Peter was not at all conscious of the Spirit's
working. Of course Peter was conscious of having heard
Christ's sermons and of having seen His miracles. But the
significance of all this just came to him at that moment. So
too when anyone accepts the Bible as the Word of God,
he is not conscious of any break in the psychological process.
He has probably been reading the Bible for some time, or as
a child he had listened to Sunday school lessons, and one
day he realizes that he believes the Bible was given by God.

The phrase "it dawned on him" is about as good a phrase
as can be found in ordinary use. Many of the theologians
compare the experience with sensation and perception. A
high school student *reasons* out his geometry problem, but
he simply *sees* the pencil and paper. Sight therefore makes
a quick contrast with reasoning. Nevertheless, when one
studies theories of sensation and learns the several ways in
which it is explained, and when sensation is distinguished
from perception, this metaphorical use of sensation to illustrate the work of the Spirit is more confusing than enlighten-
ing. It is better (so it seems to me) to say simply that God
produced the belief in the mind.

So far this exposition has been restricted to the logic of the
situation. It has been a matter of the relation between premises or reasons and conclusions. Nothing as yet has been
said about sin and its effects on man's mind. There were two
reasons for this delay. First, the logic of the situation requires discussion simply because it is a part of the subject.
It is moreover that part of the subject which has been least
discussed by theologians. They have spent most of their time
on sin, and of course this was necessary, but they have neg-

lected logic. This neglect is unfortunate because in these days it is particularly the logic that is used against the Christian position.

Christianity is often repudiated on the ground that it is circular: the Bible is authoritative because the Bible authoritatively says so. But this objection applies no more to Christianity than to any philosophic system or even to geometry. Every system of organized propositions depends of necessity on some indemonstrable premises, and every system must make an attempt to explain how these primary premises come to be accepted.

The second reason for delaying mention of sin dovetails into the first. The situation in logic remains the same, sin or no sin. Adam faced it before the fall. Of course Adam did not have a written Bible, but he was the recipient of a revelation. God spoke to him. How then could he attribute authority to God's commands? Was it possible in the garden to do what is impossible now, to demonstrate God's authority? Evidently not. To suppose so would be the same as supposing that Adam could deduce the axioms of geometry. Nor could Adam have asked Eve and taken her word for it. And surely he ought not to have appealed to Satan to establish God's authority. Rather, because God is sovereign, God's authority can be taken only on God's authority. As the Scripture says, "Because he could swear by no greater, he sware by himself" (Heb. 6:13).

THE FACTOR OF SIN

However, sin is a factor now; and although it does not alter the basic logical situation, its complications cannot go unnoticed. Furthermore, it is in relation to sin and redemption that the Bible gives some important information applicable to the question of belief in inspiration.

When Adam fell, the human race became, not *stupid* so that the truth was hard to understand, but *inimical* to the acceptance of the truth. Men did not like to retain God in their knowledge and changed the truth of God into a lie; for the carnal mind is enmity against God. Hence the preaching of the cross is to them that perish foolishness; for the natural man receiveth not the things of the Spirit of God because they are spiritually discerned. In order to accept the Gospel, therefore, it is necessary to be born again. The abnormal, depraved intellect must be remade by the Holy Spirit; the enemy must be made a friend. This is the work of regeneration; and the heart of stone can be taken away and a heart of flesh can be given only by God Himself. Resurrecting the man who is dead in sin and giving him a new life, far from being a human achievement, requires nothing less than almighty power.

It is therefore impossible by argument or preaching alone to cause anyone to believe the Bible. Only God can cause such belief. At the same time, this does not mean that argument is useless. Peter tells us "to be ready always to give an answer to every man that asketh you a reason of the hope that is in you." This was the constant practice of the apostles. Stephen disputed with the Libertines; the Jerusalem council disputed; in Ephesus Paul disputed three months in the synagogue and then continued disputing in the school of Tyrannus (Acts 6:9; 15:7; 19:8, 9; cf. Acts 17:2; 18:4, 19; 24:25). Anyone who is unwilling to argue, dispute, and reason is disloyal to his Christian duty.

At this point the natural question is, What is the use of all this expounding and explaining if it does not produce belief? The answer should be clearly understood. The witness or testimony of the Holy Spirit is a witness *to* something. The Spirit witnesses to the authority of Scripture. If no apostle or preacher expounded the message, there would be nothing in the sinner's mind for the Spirit to witness to. The Spirit cannot produce belief in Christ unless the sinner has heard of Christ. "How shall they call on him in whom they have not believed? And how shall they believe in him of whom they have not heard? So then faith cometh by hearing, and hearing by the word of God" (Rom. 10:14, 17).

No doubt God in His omnipotence could reveal the necessary information to each man individually without a written Bible or ministerial preaching. But this is not what God has done. God gave the apostles and preachers the duty of expounding the message; but the production of belief is the work of the Spirit, for faith is the gift of God.

This is part of the reason why it was said above that the best procedure for us, if we want someone to accept the doctrine of plenary and verbal inspiration, is to expound the Scripture in detail. We may well use archaeology and historical criticism too, but the main task is to communicate the message of the Bible in as understandable language as we can manage.

It is to be noted too that the sinner, without any special work of the Spirit, can understand the message. Belief in its truth and understanding its meaning are two different things. The Bible can be understood by the same methods of study used on Euclid or Aristotle. Despite some pious disclaimers, it is true that antagonistic unbelievers often enough understand the Bible better than devout Christians. The Pharisees saw the significance of Christ's claims to deity more quickly and more clearly than the disciples did.

As Paul persecuted the Christians in Jerusalem and set out for Damascus, he understood the words "Jesus is Lord" as well as any of the twelve. It was precisely because he understood so well that he persecuted so zealously. Had he been unsure of the meaning, he would not have been so exercised. But, the trouble was, he did not believe it. On the contrary, he believed that it was false. Then on the Damascus road Christ appeared to him and caused him to believe that the statement was true. Paul did not understand the phrase any better a moment after his conversion than a moment before. Doubtless in later years God revealed further information to him for use in the epistles. But at the moment, Christ did not enlarge his understanding one whit; He caused him to receive, accept, or believe what he already understood quite well. Thus it is that the Spirit witnesses to the message previously communicated.

Strong emphasis needs to be put on the work of the Holy Spirit. Man is dead in sin, an enemy of God, opposed to all righteousness and truth. He needs to be changed. Neither the preacher nor, much less, the sinner himself can cause the change. But "blessed is the man whom thou choosest, and causest to approach unto thee" (Ps. 65:4). "And I will take the stony heart out of their flesh, and will give them an heart of flesh" (Ezek. 11:19; 36:26, 27). "As many as were ordained to eternal life believed" (Acts 13:48). "God . . . when we were dead in sins, hath quickened us together with Christ" (Eph. 2:5). "For it is God which worketh in you both to will and to do of his good pleasure" (Phil. 2:13). "God hath from the beginning chosen you to salvation through santification of the Spirit and belief of the truth" (II Thess. 2:13). "Of his own will begat he us with the word of truth" (James 1:18).

These verses, which refer primarily to regeneration, are applicable to our acceptance of the Bible as the very Word of God. Indeed, the new life which the second birth initiates, the life to which we are raised from the death of sin, is precisely the life of faith; and a full faith includes the plenary and verbal inspiration of the message of salvation. It is the gift of God.

This is why the greatest of all the creeds issuing from the Reformation, the Westminster Confession, says:

"The authority of the Holy Scripture, for which it ought to be believed and obeyed, dependeth not upon the testimony of any man or church, but wholly upon God (who is truth itself), the author thereof; and therefore it is to be received because it is the Word of God.

". . . our full persuasion and assurance of the infallible truth and divine authority thereof is from the inward work of the Holy Spirit, bearing witness by and with the Word in our hearts" (I, iv and v).

In the last analysis, therefore, although historical and archaeological confirmation of the Bible's accuracy is of great interest to us and of great embarrassment to unbelievers, a conviction that the Bible is really the Word of God cannot be the conclusion of a valid argument based on more clearly evident premises. This conviction is produced by the Holy Spirit Himself.

It must always be kept in mind that the proclamation of the Gospel is part of a spiritual struggle against the supernatural powers of the Evil One, and victory comes only through the omnipotent grace of God. Accordingly, as Jesus explained His mission to both Peter and the Pharisees, so we today must expound and explain the Scripture in all its fullness to all sorts of men, and we can then be assured that our Father in Heaven will reveal His truth to some of them.

*Chapter 2*

# CAN WE BELIEVE IN THE MIRACULOUS?

*by*

FRANK O. GREEN

# Chapter 2

## CAN WE BELIEVE IN THE MIRACULOUS?

THE HISTORY OF MAN has been marked by what may be called partial thinking. Man has always had a strong tendency to follow half truths. Important examples of this tendency are with us today. For instance, some say that if only everyone had plenty of money and enough to eat and wear, all would be well and there would be no real trouble in the world. This is a large part of the Communistic philosophy. It would, of course, be very desirable if all the world's needy millions had sufficient material goods, but to say that this would be the answer to the world's problems is not true.

Another partial truth concerns science and Christianity, or the natural and the supernatural. Here again men have tended to overemphasize one part to the exclusion of the other. So the monk or religious recluse on the one hand refuses to have anything to do with the natural processes of life, except those forced upon him. On the other hand we see the so-called man of science who refuses to have anything to do with, or even recognize, anything in the universe or on the earth except that which can be measured or understood by means of the senses of touch, taste, smell, sight, and hearing.

Thus man has characteristically gone from one extreme to the other, denying either the spiritual or the natural part of his being. During the early centuries of the Christian era a large number tried to deny their natural or normal way of

life (living as hermits, holy men, monks, etc.). This re-
sulted in ridiculous practices and beliefs. Some of these actually had the support of certain church leaders, and it is
probable that one reason for the Dark Ages in Europe was
this type of thinking.

Since the beginning of modern times, men have increasingly tried to deny the spiritual part of their beings. It has
become popular to believe only in the natural and to deny
all else. During the eighteenth century clubs and other
groups were formed for the purpose of the so-called en-
lightenment of those whom they considered to be ignorant
because they retained a belief in God and the supernatural.
These groups included some of the most famous leaders of
England, the continent of Europe, and the United States.

The pendulum of partial thinking has been swinging in
the direction of a denial of the supernatural for many years
now, so that this generation finds itself near the extreme.
Although this type of partial thinking is still very prevalent,
especially in Russia and China and some other parts of the
world, there are encouraging signs that the pendulum is
starting to swing back. It is to be hoped that man's previous
experience will keep him from going to the opposite extreme
again.

The fallacy of partial thinking is of course that man shuts
himself off from the whole truth and emphasizes only a portion of it. The anecdote of the blind men who were examining an elephant is a good illustration of this kind of thinking. One man who happened to feel the side of the elephant
said, "An elephant is like a wall." Another who happened to
feel the tail said, "An elephant is like a snake." They were,
of course, both correct and honest in their statements, but
did not have the whole truth. Endless argument between
them regarding the nature of an elephant would not settle
the problem unless they were both able to obtain the whole
truth.

In the case of the blind men and the elephant, the whole truth could probably be obtained rather easily and quickly. But the problem is not so easy when dealing with some of the more important truths. The whole truth may be known, and many have found it; but unfortunately many have refused to seek for it, and have therefore not found it. The Bible says that men love darkness (or error) rather than light (or truth), because their deeds are evil.

The Bible not only tells us that if we will honestly seek the truth we will find it, it also says that we are partly of the natural and partly of the spiritual or supernatural. It tells us to render to Caesar those things that are Caesar's and to God those things that are God's. It also declares that man does not live by bread alone, but by every word that proceeds from God. The whole truth is that to be complete, man not only must accept as true what he can detect by his senses and simple reason, but must also have faith or belief in God. He must of necessity accept as true things that he cannot fully understand, and must believe them because he has been told them by a completely reliable source. This tendency of scientists and others to accept only the partial truth as represented in nature alone, gives them an incomplete basis for their thinking. We cannot therefore accept their conclusions as correct.

All of the foregoing is very important in regard to what we think about miracles. It is logical that if we are governed only by the laws of nature, we have no basis for belief in anything that we would call miraculous. But if the laws of nature do not constitute the entire picture, we may logically include miracles as a necessary part of the complete whole.

### Purpose of Miracles

It is no coincidence that all miracles recorded in the Bible fit into the pattern of the whole. That is, Christ never performed a miracle by making a man with five legs, but He did perform a miracle whereby man's useless legs were made useful again. He never performed a miracle whereby a creature was produced having grotesque organs on the outside of the body, but He did heal or restore the use of organs inside the body that were not functioning properly. The virgin birth was accomplished by co-operating with or working with the laws of nature which man correctly recognizes as true and reliable. However, in the virgin birth means were used which we do not yet know about or understand, but which we cannot logically, on that account alone, exclude from what we call truth. It is not logical to expect or assume that God is restricted in His doings to the laws that are understood by us at present.

If someone does not believe in God at all, he is arbitrarily cutting himself off from an understanding of the whole truth, and we should remember that his conclusions are to be judged on that basis. If he does not believe in God, we should expect that he will not believe in what are often called miracles and we should realize that this disbelief is a logical result of his refusal to believe in God. A belief in miracles follows from a belief in God.

It is necessary that all true Christians believe in such miracles as the incarnation, the virgin birth, the resurrection, since these are among the chief tenets of our Christian faith. If these miracles were not true, there is no such thing as Christianity and no one can accurately be called a Christian.

A second kind of miracle mentioned in the Bible, such as healing, the raising of Lazarus from the dead, and the like, is not required as a basis for our salvation, but was for the purpose of proving the reality of Christ's words, so that men might believe in Him. It is here that the greatest problem regarding the belief in miracles usually arises. Likewise it is here that we should exercise the greatest caution. This is especially true since members of the Christian church through the centuries have at various times claimed to have performed or to have observed miracles. Just as the genuine has been imitated in other lines of endeavor, so we should expect imitators here also. An early attempt at imitation is spoken of in the Bible where the disciples were actually offered money if they would disclose their supposed secret regarding the successful performing of miracles (Acts 8: 9-24).

## Stumbling Blocks to Acceptance of Miracles

A reliable test for determining whether or not a miracle is real is the one set forth by Scripture: Was the so-called miracle performed for the glory of God and to extend His kingdom, or was it for the glory or monetary profit of some man or organization of men? It is the writer's opinion that most of the so-called miracles performed since the time Christ and the apostles have not been actually performed, but only claimed to have been performed. It is of course possible that the claims of some lady that she miraculously found her best thimble with the aid of St. Anthony are true, but it is quite unlikely, and whether we believe the story or not has little to do with whether or not we are Christians. But as Christians we must be convinced that if God in His wisdom wishes to perform miracles today by whatever means He chooses, it is certainly possible for Him to do so.

Another great stumbling block that many have encountered in considering the subject of miracles is their inability to correlate the miraculous with the invariant character of the laws of nature that they see about them. This is perhaps more true of those who have studied science and performed scientific experiments than of others.

The scientist becomes more and more convinced of two points as he studies and makes experiments with natural laws. First, that the well-established laws (such as the Law of Gravity) are dependable. Secondly, absolutely that one cannot always reliably predict results because there are laws that are not known or well understood. This is called the scientific method or attitude, and the experienced scientist has been confirmed in it as a result of a life of experimentation. The scientific method is very useful and has been very productive when applied in the natural realm. But the natural realm does not include the whole of truth or reality.

The reason why thinkers such as Hume of a former day and many scientists of today who are not Christians reject the possibility of any miracle ever happening is because they are rendering judgment from the standpoint of natural phenomena only. In following this course they are unconsciously supporting the truth that God's laws of nature are invariant and absolutely dependable, but by their refusal to believe in God who is a spirit, they are making invalid any conclusions that they may reach except those having to do with natural phenomena.

### Necessity of a Belief in God

So then a very important difference between a Christian and a non-Christian is that the Christian accepts the fact that the whole man includes both a spiritual being and a physical being which can be known by the five senses, and that belief in God is absolutely necessary to an understanding of truth in its entirety.

The aim of much of this chapter so far has been to establish the fact that correct thinking regarding miracles is absolutely impossible if one limits himself only to part of the truth. If one refuses to accept the fact that there is more to truth than that which can be known by the five senses, no amount of persuasion will avail and further reading in this chapter will be useless. There are, however, many excellent and logical reasons for accepting and believing this fact. Nevertheless, when all is said and done, the starting point is belief.

Blaise Pascal, a famous seventeenth-century scientist, well

known for his statement of Pascal's law in physics and for certain important mathematical derivations, emphasized the importance of belief in God: "God has given man enough reasons in nature and his surroundings to believe in Him if he will believe, and also enough reasons to disbelieve in Him if he will not believe." Pascal wrote also that "God desires belief and that if He would show Himself completely to man, the result would not be belief but terror." In the Revelation (6:16, 17) we read that in the day of judgment many people will cry to the mountains and rocks, "Fall on us, and hide us from the face of him that sitteth on the throne, and from the wrath of the Lamb: for the great day of his wrath is come; and who shall be able to stand?" At that time there will be no question in anyone's mind regarding the truths of God; all will believe. But that will not be a time of true belief but of terror.

The devil is logical in continually attacking the veracity of the Bible by various means. It is obvious that if man can be tricked into believing that the Bible is untrue, or is partly true, or is filled with fables, then man's acceptance of its truths will be undermined and thus any adequate basis for belief will be removed. But there is abundant reason for believing the Bible; for its original documentation equals or surpasses that of any other historical activity commonly accepted as true. If one has sincere doubt in this regard, he has only to study the facts concerning original or early Biblical manuscripts, including the Dead Sea Scrolls and such like.

A type of acceptance or belief which is common is illustrated by man's belief in atoms. No educated person, scientist or non-scientist, discredits the statement that there are atoms. However, no scientist or non-scientist has ever seen an atom, and it is extremely unlikely that anyone ever will. Why then do we believe that there are atoms? The non-scientists believe because they believe the scientists, and the scientists believe because their experiments require it. If then we can believe the scientists who specifically affirm the truths regarding atoms which they have never seen but which they believe in because of many and abundant proofs, why should we refuse to believe the men of the Bible who likewise had many and abundant proofs? In both cases those whose statements and observations are to be believed, are recognized as specialists in their fields and give abundant evidence that they have searched exhaustively into the matter of which they speak. It is unfortunately true that some non-Christian scientists occasionally attempt to speak with authority about spiritual matters of which they have little knowledge. It should be recognized that in this case they are not speaking with the authority with which they speak of scientific matters.

In emphasizing the necessity for belief we must continually keep in mind that the most learned are abysmally ignorant compared to God. Moreover, history offers abundant proof that following man's thoughts and reasonings only, and refusing to believe in and follow the thoughts and reasonings of God, always results in disaster.

Logical thinking demands belief in God as a necessary part of all human activity. In fact, we must conclude that one is either illogical, supremely egotistical or a fool who maintains that he knows it all and that therefore there is no place for belief in his life.

Unfortunately many scientists, because of their preoccupation with physical and natural phenomena, have taken the one-sided view that belief in spiritual things is not necessary. They are of course incomplete and illogical in this position since they have an unbalanced view of truth. But because of the great impact of science and its findings on modern living, they have been followed by many people who do not realize that they cannot speak with authority on spiritual matters.

I submit then that all who disbelieve in God and spiritual things are incomplete and illogical. But scientists are perhaps more illogical than some others in that they understand the laws of experimentation better and are accustomed to applying critical thinking to data to extract the real meaning. Even though they are scientists, they are also men, and thus are attempting to deny a part of their make-up.

I have great respect for the work of all true scientists and do not in any way mean to depreciate their discoveries of the various laws of God, nor to minimize their importance to the progress of mankind. But after many years spent in the study of science and in meeting with scientists and scientific organizations, I believe the conclusion is inescapable that all scientists, from the greatest to the least, are but men, and thus speak only as men and not as God. It has also become increasingly evident that the findings of science, wonderful as they are in their rightful place, do not represent ultimate truth, and that faith in God is an absolutely essential requirement of all who wish to be free from this form of partial thinking and who are seeking the whole truth.

### Nature of Miracle and Its Acceptance

In his book *Miracles,* C. S. Lewis explains clearly and logically that miracles should be expected in our world which includes both the spiritual and the material. This involves the question as to what we mean by the word *miracle.*

Unfortunately this word usually means, even to many Christians, that God is interfering in some way with the laws of nature and thus upsetting an established order for no good reason, perhaps merely in a spirit of caprice. This does not fit in with their idea of God, and rightly so; therefore they refuse to accept the possibility of miracles.

A second reason some Christians do not believe in the possibility of miracles is that they have carelessly allowed themselves to be influenced by the ideas and beliefs of the world, which does not accept the fact of God.

A third reason some Christians do not believe in miracles is that it often seems to them as though God is being summoned by some church or religious order or some man, just as Aladdin summoned the genie to perform an unusual thing so that they can make more money or become more famous or receive some personal benefit. People are, of course, right in rejecting as not genuine such so-called miracles, regardless of how large the church or religious order which claims them. But these false claims and attempts to capitalize on gullible people are not adequate reasons for rejecting the truly miraculous, just as we do not refuse to use a genuine dollar bill because we know that there are counterfeits.

The Christian should remind himself that God created and understands completely the biochemistry of the body, and that He chose as part of His great and wise plan to use this knowledge to raise a Lazarus from the dead or to heal the man sick of palsy. This is not caprice but is part of the good and loving plan of God. We should realize that it is only from man's position of ignorance that these acts look like events that are out of order or setting, and in his pride and egotism man is judging God's action by saying so. From God's viewpoint they are all part of the correct and established order in His universe.

So then it is proposed that the correct meaning of the word *miracle* is that God is doing something in His plan for His universe which we do not understand, or which seems to us to be out of the ordinary or unusual, or has not been done very often before.

For clarity let us consider an example. A missionary goes into a jungle carrying a portable radio transmitter. On a certain day he cranks the generator and calls the mission base, asking that they send supplies via airplane at a certain time. It would seem to the men of the jungle to be a miracle when the airplane appears on schedule with the supplies. Likewise we in our ignorance often tend to consider things as miracles because of our ignorance of God's purposes and actions.

To the Christian then a belief in miracles is perfectly logical, since he has faith in God and has some concept of His might and majesty and power and eternal purposes, and believes that anything is possible with Him.

We do not think it miraculous when, after putting wheat grains into the ground in the spring, we see green shoots coming out of the dirt. But we call it a miracle when Christ takes five loaves and two fishes and uses them to feed five thousand people. From our standpoint the latter is a miracle, but from God's viewpoint both instances are multiplications of food, one by a method that we human beings partly understand or are familiar with, and one by a method that we don't understand and are not familiar with.

In conclusion then, the confusion regarding God and miracles and spiritual things has several origins, not the least of which is the intense activity of our enemy the devil. His ability to create and promote confusion is often unsuspected but real in its effects. His efforts are especially successful among those who do not realize that they are blind to the true situation.

Just as men are superior to animals and matter, so God is superior to man, and thus it is completely illogical to assume that God in His actions is subject to what we can understand with our finite minds. So we see that men are illogical or dishonest or foolish who, by their refusal to believe in God, claim omniscience for themselves and declare that there cannot be miracles.

We should be cautioned here, however, as in the field of

science or any other field of thought. We must think carefully and critically, and continually seek direction from the Lord who has promised to guide us in all our ways. Moreover here, as in all other fields of thought or human endeavor, there are many counterfeits and we should be careful not to be hoodwinked into accepting them as the real thing.

Nevertheless, we conclude by reaffirming that Christians have a completely adequate and entirely logical basis for believing in miracles and that a belief in miracles should follow.

*Chapter 3*

# DOES SCIENCE CONTRADICT THE BIBLE?

*by*

EDSON R. PECK

# Chapter 3

# DOES SCIENCE CONTRADICT THE BIBLE?

## *Importance of the Question*

THE QUESTION OF CONFLICT between the Bible and science owes its importance to the tremendous influence of these two factors in human life, and particularly in our Western culture. Laws have been established, institutions have arisen, family life has been patterned and individual lives are still being transformed through the influence of Biblical Christianity. Modern science, on the other hand, has revolutionized the physical aspects of man's living in those areas of the world where it has flourished, conferring the benefits and problems of modern technology. Beyond these effects of the Bible and of science upon human living are their effects upon man's understanding of the universe and of himself. Each deals in its own way with basic reality or truth; each opens to the mind enormous and awe-inspiring vistas for contemplation.

Any conflict between the Bible and science is a conflict, real or supposed, between authorities; for the Bible has long been regarded as an authority while science, its inner principles inaccessible without long training, speaks through its scholars as a religion through priests. A conflict between authorities is sure to enlist on one side or another many who make their decision from loyalty and not from reason, while it leaves some undecided in mental confusion.

The high school or college student from a Christian home may be troubled or shaken in his faith by the authoritative aspect of human learning. It is imperative for him to gain a reasonable perspective of the relationship of the intellectual with the spiritual world. Likewise in evangelism, as the church or the individual believer presses the authority of Jesus Christ by using the Scriptures, a discussion of the compatibility of science and the Bible is helpful in arousing interest and meeting natural objections.

An illustration of the result that may come from the apparent conflict of authority is the case of Einstein. In his autobiography, Einstein records a brief but ecstatic religious experience in boyhood which was displaced by unbelief when the reading of books convinced him that many things in the Bible could not be true. He never again professed religious faith, although his mind was not closed on the matter.

### *Does a Conflict Exist?*

The answer to this question concerning conflict is negative is one sense and positive in another. First, it is the writer's deep conviction that *no basic conflict* does exist between the Bible and science. Within its proper sphere, neither contradicts the other. They are supplementary. One can honestly and fearlessly be both a scientist and a Christian. He can accept the Bible as inspired by God and at the same time join in man's search for knowledge by experimentation combined with reasoning. This answer remains essentially that given by Sir Francis Bacon, appearing on the flyleaf of Darwin's *Origin of Species:* "To conclude, therefore, let no man out of a weak conceit of sobriety, or an ill-applied moderation, think or maintain that a man can search too far or be too well studied in the book of God's Word, or in the book of God's works; divinity or philosophy; but rather let men endeavor an endless progress or proficience in both."[1]

There have been, nevertheless, many bitter attacks by

[1]Francis Bacon, *Advancement of Learning,* First Book, I, 3.

scientists, or in the name of science, upon the Bible. It must not be forgotten that the reverse has been equally true. Two quotations will suffice to illustrate the debate and antagonism which have often occurred, initiated both by scientists and theologians.

Sir Julian Huxley:

> Darwinism removed the whole idea of God as the creator of organisms from the sphere of rational discussion.[2]

Bacon:

> . . . natural philosophy has, in every age, met with a troublesome and difficult opponent: I mean superstition, and a blind and immoderate zeal for religion. For we see that, among the Greeks, those who first disclosed the natural causes of thunder and storms to the yet untrained ears of men were condemned as guilty of impiety toward the gods. Nor did some of the old fathers of Christianity treat those much better who showed by the most positive proofs (such as no one now disputes) that the earth is spherical, and thence asserted that there were antipodes.[3]

It is clear from these complementary quotations that conflicts do arise between science and Christianity. It may be observed, however, that these conflicts arise whenever a scholar makes a pronouncement outside his own field of learning. When science becomes a religion, or religion dictates scientific thought, there is trouble.

### *The Basic Principle*

The foregoing considerations lead to the basic principle of harmony between Biblical Christianity and science. It is that each authority is to be respected in its own area. In spite of its simplicity, this principle needs some elaboration.

[2]Sol Tax, editor, *Evolution after Darwin* (Chicago: The University of Chicago Press), III, 45.
[3]Bacon, *Novum Organum,* First Book, p. 91.

First, what is the area of the Bible's authority? Unlimited, one might say, for does not the Bible claim to be inspired, "God-breathed"? And if God be the Author, even though His Word be given through human personalities, must not the authority of the Bible be absolute? The answer is in the very text just quoted: "All scripture is God-breathed and is profitable for doctrine, for reproof, for correction, for instruction in righteousness, that the man of God may be capable, equipped for every good work" (II Tim. 3:16, 17). Here the uses of Scripture are indicated to be spiritual and moral in nature.

Consider other texts on the subject of the purposes of Scripture: "These are written, that ye might believe that Jesus is the Christ, the Son of God; and that believing ye might have life through his name" (John 20:31). "The secret things belong unto the Lord our God: but those things which are revealed belong unto us and to our children for ever, that we may do all the words of this law" (Deut. 29:29). "The law of the Lord is perfect, converting the soul: the testimony of the Lord is sure, making wise the simple" (Ps. 19:7).

It is clear that the Bible is not given to teach men all knowledge, but specifically to teach "all things that pertain unto life and godliness" (II Peter 1:3). By this very fact, the Bible is *not* a textbook of science. The aim of a textbook of science is to teach fact and reasoning without regard to its implications. This self-imposed limitation of the Bible is well stated by Bacon:[4]

> Some . . . have pretended to find the truth of all natural philosophy in the Scriptures; scandalizing and traducing all other philosophy as heathenish and profane. But there is no such enmity between God's Word and His works; neither do they give honour to the Scriptures as they suppose, but much imbase them. For to seek

[4]Bacon, *Advancement of Learning*, Second Book, XXV, 16.

heaven and earth in the word of God, whereof it is said "Heaven and earth shall pass, but my word shall not pass," is to seek temporary things among eternal: and as to seek divinity in philosophy is to seek the living amongst the dead, so to seek philosophy in divinity is to seek the dead amongst the living.

More pithy but to the same point is the comment of Cardinal Baronius (1538–1607): "The Holy Spirit intended to teach us in the Bible how to go to heaven, not how the heavens go."[5]

As to the area of the authority of science, one may listen to Newton, a devout man as well as one of the foremost scientists of all time. In his Rules of Reasoning in Natural Philosophy,[6] he lays down two principles:

I. We are to admit no more causes of natural things than are both true and sufficient to explain their appearance.

II. Therefore to the same natural effects we must, as far as possible, assign the same causes.

For our purposes science will be defined as the study of natural things, that is, of the physical world. One task of science is to observe nature rather than to imagine or to accept tradition for what phenomena exist. This simple statement has a far-reaching corollary. To be a proper object of scientific study, either a phenomenon must be repeatable under experimentation; or else, if like the geological history of the earth or the visit of a non-periodic comet, it cannot be reproduced, a phenomenon must be sufficiently documented. It is clear that the science of unique or non-repeatable phenomena is necessarily less well founded than experimental science. The former involves two questions not involved in the latter, the reliability of the documentation, and the limited and possibly scanty nature of the evidence.

[5]Quoted by Galileo in his "Letter to the Grand Duchess Christine of Lorraine." Compare *Great Books of the Western World* (1952), 28, 126.
[6]Isaac Newton, *Principia Mathematica*.

A particular concern of science mentioned in Newton's Rules is to clarify relationships of cause and effect among natural phenomena. In so doing, science destroys superstitions. Superstition proposes for the cause of natural phenomena the undefined, the irrational, or the imagined. Science substitutes demonstration for superstition, showing that physical phenomena in all their overwhelming complexity and variety conform to a very few postulates of wide or apparently universal validity. These postulates are called physical laws or laws of nature; but it is helpful to realize that they are man-made. They are man's description of his observations of nature.

The laws of nature must therefore not be considered sacred in themselves. It should be understood that scientific laws have varying degrees of accuracy and varying areas of validity. For example, Newton's laws of mechanics are highly exact for ordinary motions; but as velocities become comparable to the speed of light, these laws give place to the mechanics of special relativity. Sometimes laws are so completely verified as to be beyond question; sometimes the term *law* is applied from personal bias to one of several hypotheses which equally well account for what is observed.

Now in terms of the basic principle of respect for Christianity and science in the area of each, one may summarize the situation as follows. First, as between neighboring states, there may be border disputes, that is, disagreements as to where the boundary properly lies. In the extreme case, just as one country may aspire to world dominion, so scientists or Christians may deny any territory to the other. The denial of any proper area for science hardly concerns us today; it may properly be called ignorance or bigotry. The converse occurrence is fairly frequent: a number of scientists seek to make a religion of science. Next, there are areas which are common to science and Christianity. The Bible speaks of creation, and so does cosmology. The Bible speaks of man, and so does psychology. Finally, the concept of separate or overlapping areas of science and Christianity implies that each field supplements and enriches the other. The following paragraphs will discuss some of these topics in detail.

### The Religion of Science

The efforts of some to make a religion out of science may be exemplified by these excerpts from the Darwin Centennial Convocation address of Sir Julian Huxley on November 26, 1959. It is worth quoting to show the uncompromising nature of such attempts:[7]

> The broad outlines of the new evolutionary picture of ultimates are beginning to be visible. Man's destiny is to be the sole agent for the future evolution of this planet. . . . It is only through possessing a mind that he has become the dominant portion of this planet and the agent responsible for its evolution: and it will be only by the right use of that mind that he will be able to exercise that responsibility rightly. . . . And he must face it unaided by outside help. In the evolutionary pattern of thought there is no longer either need or room for the supernatural. . . . Evolutionary man can no longer take refuge from his loneliness in the arms of a divinized father-figure whom he has himself created. . . . Our feet still drag in the biological mud, even when we lift our heads into the conscious air. But, unlike those remote ancestors of ours, we can truly see something of the promised land beyond. We can do so with the aid of a new instrument of vision—our rational, knowledge-based imagination. . . . Our new organization of thought —belief-system, framework of values, ideology, call it what you will—must grow and be developed in the light of our new evolutionary vision. . . . The only way in which the present split between religion and science

[7]Tax, Vol. III, pp. 254 ff.

could be mended would be through the acceptance by
science of the fact and value of religion as an organ of
evolving man and the acceptance by religion that religions do and must evolve.

A critical discussion of these opinions of Sir Julian would
be unjust without quoting the entire text. It is evident, however, that he speaks as a seer, not as a scientist: he himself
uses the word *imagination*. From the logical viewpoint, his
denial of God's existence can only be a matter of faith, just
as is my affirmation of God's existence; for no man can claim
omniscience. He ignores the historic basis of Christianity
which distinguishes it from all other religions, centering
about the appearance of Jesus Christ in history and His
resurrection. One might also note that he uses the word
*responsibility*, while explicitly doing away with the One in
whom all responsibility finds its meaning. Clearly, this religion of Sir Julian's is completely anti-Christian; but equally
clearly, it is not the statement of science but of a scientist.
Its pronouncements extend completely beyond demonstration.

### Natural or Spiritual?

Questions of the exact boundary between science and
Christianity are not especially pertinent to the present discussion, although they may be interesting. Here there are
matters which are little understood on either side, and issues
are often obscured in technical jargon or different ways of
using the same word. For example, in what sense does God
actively sustain the material creation? What is actually
meant by the words "by him all things consist" (Col. 1:17)
or "upholding all things by the word of his power" (Heb.
1:3)? Is it true that, as the gospel song says, "It took a miracle to put the stars in place; it took a miracle to hang the
world in space"? Or was there an original miracle in which

all matter was created in enormously hot and condensed form, and did the universe then unfold itself according to the properties with which God had endowed matter? Again, where is the boundary between psychiatry and the work of the Holy Spirit? How is the physical brain related to the immortal spirit? These questions are typical of those which do not involve actual conflict between science and Christianity, for definitive answers cannot be given.

### Science in the Bible

It is necessary now to turn our attention to overlapping areas between the Bible and science. This common territory occurs because the Bible does make certain statements about the physical world in very definite terms. No inconsistency is involved here with the statement that the purposes of the Bible are primarily moral and spiritual. On the contrary, the scientific statements made by the Bible are those which have moral and spiritual implications. The Bible teaches that God, whose existence is without beginning or end, created the physical universe "in the beginning" (Gen. 1:1)—that is, in the beginning of time as we know it. The age of the universe is therefore finite. The physical world is derivative, not primary: it was made apparently from nothing by the word of God. On this foundation, the Bible teaches that the meaning and purpose of the universe are to be found only in God and His plans which center in Jesus Christ, that God transcends the physical universe, and that all belongs to God (Gen. 1:1; Heb. 11:3; John 1:2; Col. 1:16; Heb. 1:2; I Kings 8:27; I Chron. 29:14).

The Bible teaches that God prepared this world for mankind, and that in a special act of creation He created man upon it. These statements form the necessary base for many teachings: God's providential care; our entire responsibility and debt of gratitude, love and service to Him; the common sinful condition of all men, and the salvation offered in com-

mon to all men; our responsibility to all men; our capability
of companionship with God; our immortal soul. The Bible
teaches that God brought a flood in judgment upon a corrupt
race. From this it proceeds to show that God is patient but
also that He will surely punish sin with judgment.

The moral force of these Biblical statements may best be
appreciated by considering the consequences of their renun-
ciation. These were well put by Professor George Gaylord
Simpson at the Chicago meeting of the American Association
for Advancement of Science in 1959. Professor Simpson is
quoted as follows:

> Man has no special status other than his definition as
> a distinct species of animal. . . . It is no more true that
> fruits, for instance, were made for the delectation of man
> than that man evolved for the delectation of tigers. . . .
> Man is responsible to himself and for himself. "Himself"
> here means the whole human species. . . . The future of
> mankind is dim indeed—if there is any future.[8]

We proceed to discuss very briefly two of these questions,
the creation of the universe and the origin of man. They are
in contrast, since in one case science seems to be in agreement with Scripture, while in the other case the reverse opinion is the usual one. The reader must refer to other sources
for detailed expositions. A good survey of thought in these
areas is *The Christian View of Science and the Scripture*
by Bernard Ramm.[9]

### Creation

The Biblical affirmation concerning the fact of creation is
in complete harmony with scientific facts and laws as they
are presently known. A few of the lines of evidence are as
follows. The second law of thermodynamics, which has been
called "time's arrow," requires a one-way progression from

[8]The author culled these quotations from a report in the *Saturday Review*
on the Darwin Centennial meeting in Chicago, 1959.

[9]Bernard Ramm, *The Christian View of Science and the Scripture* (Grand
Rapids: Wm. B. Eerdmans Publishing Co., 1954).

a highly organized condition in which matter and energy are localized to a disorganized state in which temperature and density differences disappear. In this sense the universe is running down; it cannot therefore be infinitely old. The stars radiate their energy; it must eventually be exhausted, so the process cannot have been eternal. Radioactive atoms exist in nature; these must have been formed a finite time ago, or all would by now have undergone their spontaneous decay which leads eventually to stable atoms. The red shift of light from distant galaxies appears to indicate an over-all expansion of the universe; and this extrapolated backwards leads one to postulate an initial explosion of the known universe from a single mass of enormously condensed and hot matter.

All this being said, it must be noted that not all scientists accept the idea of an actual time of beginning for the physical world. Some postulate a pulsating universe which will again condense and repeat the process; others suppose as yet unknown processes of continuous creation. Gigantic radio telescopes are in use and under construction partly to shed further light on such cosmological processes. A report in *Time* magazine of February 24, 1961, tells of evidence from the radio telescope at Cambridge University supporting the postulate of an explosion starting the universe on its expansion some eight billion years ago.

The Christian may not be cocksure and complacent in considering this quest of science. It is encouraging and fascinating but not crucial that the weight of evidence at present indicates a time of creation. After all, the Bible does not say when or just how "the beginning" was. In the last analysis, this is a matter of faith.

### Man

The Bible specifically speaks of man as a special creation; not descended from animals, but made from the ground and endowed by God with qualities somehow resembling His own (Gen. 1:26, 27; 2:7). This is one point on which it appears that the majority of scientists are in opposition to the statement of Scripture. Their position is not surprising nor alarming to the Christian. It is to be expected that in our times a man with scientific habits and without a strong personal belief in God would adopt the postulate that man is a mere product of nature, in preference to the only alternative, that man is a special creation. It indeed seems true that life has appeared in the course of a long process, the higher forms coming later. Incidentally, one may wonder how Moses also knew of this progression unless Genesis 1 were inspired. Given also the extensive researches of Darwin and his ingenuity in suggesting the mechanism of natural selection, the prevailing scientific opinion appears inevitable.

It is reasonable, however, to question the conclusion of the majority of scientists in this matter. One may make several reasonable queries. Do the facts rule out the possibility of man's special creation? Do all the facts support the postulate of the evolution of man? Is the proposed mechanism of natural selection adequate? It would seem that the answers to the first two questions are negative, while the third is a matter of debate. The facts do not require denial of creation; rather, scientists find the possibility of a theory not requiring an act of God. There are facts suggesting special creation, particularly in the enormous gap between animals and man in intellectual and moral areas. The following statements are not typical, but it is significant that they were made at the Darwin Centennial in 1959 to which reference has already been made:

MacDonald Critchley, senior physician, National Hospital, London:

> There is evidence that speech was an endowment of *pithecanthropos*. . . . Between these (animal sounds)

and human articulate speech lies a very considerable gulf. Even in the case of the most untutored, primitive and savage human communities the language-system is so far removed in its complexity from the crude and simple utterances of the sagest of the animals as to be hardly comparable. And nowhere and at no time has there been any hint of an approximation between these two extremes. No "missing link" between animal and human communication has yet been identified.

Can it be, therefore, that a veritable Rubicon does exist between animals and man after all. . . ?[10]

A. R. Wallace, a contemporary of Charles Darwin and an independent proponent of the postulate of natural selection, is quoted as follows:

Natural selection could only have endowed the savage with a brain a little superior to that of the ape, whereas he actually possesses one but very little inferior to that of the average members of our learned societies.[11]

As to man's moral nature, one may simply remark that a most notable difference exists between man and animals, to man's disadvantage. Man indeed appears capable of a deliberate cruelty and a degree of debauchery unknown among animals.

It is interesting to note that the adequacy of natural selection is sometimes questioned even in the case of animal development. Everett C. Olson, professor of Geology at the University of Chicago, made this statement at the Darwin centennial:

The variety of phenomena (in paleontology) and the opposing features of many of them appear to require manipulation of the available mechanisms to degrees that seem almost incredible.

Perhaps this is illusion and there are, in fact, no prob-

---

[10]Tax, Vol. II, pp. 305 ff.
[11]*Ibid.*, Vol. II, p. 310.

lems. Possibly this is the case, but it seems no more subject to demonstration than does the contrary proposition. If problems do exist, it is difficult to devise methods of approaching solutions. We are then in the position of believing, without definite proof, that factors beyond these recognized at present are of major importance in some areas of evolution, but of not knowing just what they are or how they may be discovered. This is an unfortunate, negative situation.[12]

One may conclude that while belief in man's special creation is unpopular, it is not properly unscientific. It might be highly profitable both for science and the propagation of Christianity for more Christians to enter the interesting fields of geology, anthropology, paleontology and biology, which touch upon the nature of man and the history of the world; it would certainly be more profitable than mere defensive debate.

### Concord

We conclude that a scientist may be a Christian, and conversely, that a Christian may be a scientist, without compromising that which properly belongs to each of these areas of life and thought. We conclude also that a Christian layman may rely on the Bible as God's inerrant revelation, but that in dealing with scientific questions he needs a degree of humility and a willingness to examine evidence.

There is much that can be said in the positive sense as to the concord of science and the Bible. Both combat superstition. For an example of this in Scripture, read Isaiah 44:9-20. In the Bible, the scientist finds his charter. The Bible states the uniformity of natural phenomena and indicates that it is an honorable thing to study God's works. In the Bible he finds also the answers to those questions

[12]*Ibid.,* Vol. I, p. 542.

which science cannot settle: questions of ultimate causes, reasons and goals; questions related to man's deeper needs. Conversely, science adds a new dimension to the understanding of God's greatness and wisdom.

*Chapter 4*

# WHAT BOOKS BELONG IN THE CANON OF SCRIPTURE?

*by*

R. LAIRD HARRIS

## Chapter 4

# WHAT BOOKS BELONG IN THE CANON OF SCRIPTURE?*

WHEN WE SPEAK of the canon of Scripture, we spell it with a single "n." This canon has nothing to do with artillery! It comes from an old Greek word meaning "rule" or "standard." The study of the canon of Scripture is the study of the process by which the books of the Bible became recognized as true and as the authoritative standard of the church.

### Why Study the Canon?

From one point of view it may seem unnecessary to study the canon. Others have done a good job on it already. Our Bible of sixty-six books has been approved by untold millions of Christians, both careful scholars and ordinary laymen. We could just take it as it is.

And this might be a good conclusion—though it would probably be a bad argument. For from this point of view it would be unnecessary to study many things. For instance, why study geometry? The same old theorems have been demonstrated by generations of high school students since Pythagoras squared his hypotenuse! But it seems helpful for us to learn for ourselves the wisdom of the ancients. Therefore a Christian who wants to know these things for himself should study all over again the evidence for the reception of our sixty-six sacred books.

*For a fuller development of this subject, see the author's *Inspiration and Canonicity of the Bible* (Grand Rapids: Zondervan Publishing House, 1957).

Furthermore, although Christians have for many years been in agreement on our sixty-six books, there are some who do not agree. First, there are the Roman Catholics. Since the Middle Ages, the Roman Church has believed in the so-called apocryphal books as well as our sixty-six. These apocryphal books are fourteen extra books or additions to Biblical books probably written after Malachi and before Matthew. We shall have something to say about them later.

Secondly, there are many people not Christians who spend their time thinking up objections to the Bible. They do not accept Jesus Christ as Saviour and therefore could hardly be expected to believe in the book that tells about His saving work. Most of them really do not know much about Christianity or its origin. They vaguely suppose that the Bible was the product of early ignorance or superstition or both. It is helpful, when we meet such people, to be able to press home the truths of the Gospel. Sometimes they will let us say something on these points that may help them—only we must have something to say!

Finally, there are unbelievers, modernists in the churches and teachers in schools who really have studied these things more or less. Sometimes such men approach the subject from the viewpoint of unbelief and are led to unjustified conclusions. It is important in listening to them to be able to distinguish fact from fancy. If someday you have to sit under such a teacher, you can keep your feet on the ground better if you have a few facts in your head!

### The Old Testament Canon

There was a time when there was no Old Testament canon. We ourselves feel so blessed with our Bible that we forget that apparently there was none before Moses. God spoke to our first parents and to the patriarchs directly. Abraham was a prophet (Gen. 20:7) and he spoke for God to others around him. But God had not yet given a written revelation.

It remained for Moses to write the first part of the Old Testament, the first five books. We call these the Pentateuch (five books). The Jews call them the Torah (the Law). The Bible many times calls them the Law of Moses.

In the last one hundred years or more, the Mosaic authorship of the Pentateuch has been heavily attacked. A German named Wellhausen popularized a theory that the Pentateuch was a patchwork of documents put together a thousand years after Moses and of no great reliability. He called the four principal documents J, E, D, and P after special characteristics he found in each document. Those who followed him insisted that one could always identify the P document (P for priestly) by its attention to such things as dates, chronology, genealogies. They did not seem to notice that the P document has all the dates because those critics who separated out the P document put all the dates in it! It is like dividing a box of candy into creams and nuts and then pouting because there are no nuts among the creams! Fortunately, further study and the newer discoveries of archaeology have shown Wellhausen missed the mark by several yards, and now the destructive critics are forging a whole new crop of theories to show why Moses could not have written the Pentateuch. This is not our study just now. For our present purposes, we may be satisfied with the word of Christ. He declared that we should believe Moses and his writings, and He repeatedly said that Moses wrote the Pentateuch (John 5:46, 47; Luke 16:31; 24:44; etc.).

Moses' writings were a big step toward the formation of the Old Testament canon. The Pentateuch is about a fourth of the Old Testament. But how did the people of antiquity know these books were canonical? As a matter of fact, some didn't. Korah, Dathan, and Abiram (Num. 16) did not think much of Moses. But then the earth opened and swallowed them alive, and this was a big lesson to Korah, Dathan, and

Abiram. Miriam on one occasion also objected to her brother.
God visited her with leprosy for seven days. What we are
saying is that God gave such supernatural signs to accom-
pany Moses that his prophetic office was beyond doubt. Indeed, to doubt this part of the canon in those days was
dangerous! God declared Moses was a prophet and a special
one, and said that Miriam and the others should have feared
to speak against him (Num. 12:6-8).

Joshua evidently accepted Moses' Law as canonical (Josh.
1:7, 8). Later leaders also add their testimony. Amaziah
spared the children of those who assassinated his father
(II Kings 14:6) as it was commanded in the Law of Moses
(Deut. 24:16). Hezekiah kept the commandments which
the Lord gave Moses (II Kings 18:6). When the book of
the Law was found in the temple, Josiah recognized and
obeyed it as the Law of Moses (II Kings 23:25). The
Psalms and Prophets quote from it repeatedly. It was the
beginning of the canon.

In a book called Ecclesiasticus (not our Ecclesiastes) written about 180 B.C., Joshua is called the "successor of Moses
in prophecies." This fits Deuteronomy 18:15-22 where God
told Moses that He would raise up a line of prophets finally
ending in Christ the great Prophet. So God revealed Himself to Joshua (Josh. 5:13-15) and it is proper to call Joshua a
prophet. We are not absolutely sure that Joshua wrote the
book that bears his name, for the New Testament nowhere
expressly says so, but this is the old Jewish tradition. The
book is classified with the prophets by the Jews and by the
New Testament. First Kings 16:34 speaks of Joshua as a
prophet.

The next book, Judges, was combined with Ruth in all the
old Jewish sources. We do not know who wrote Judges-Ruth,
but it seems likely that it was done by someone in the time
of Samuel, perhaps by Samuel himself. It too is classified
among the prophets by the Jews and the New Testament.

## ONE STORY—MANY WRITERS

One point we must stress here is that these books were not considered as separate histories, but were part of a continued story to which different prophets added various sections. Occasionally you see the Bible pictured as a five-foot shelf of books with Genesis, Exodus, Leviticus, Numbers and Deuteronomy standing together; then, after a space, come the twelve books of history, etc. This is not the true picture at all. Jesus and the apostles referred to the Old Testament as a unit. They usually called it the "law and the prophets" or just "the law." It was indeed written by various prophets, but they all spoke "as they were moved by the Holy Ghost" (II Peter 1:21). It is all one volume and its principal author is God the Holy Spirit.

This concept gives us the main Protestant principle of canonicity. What is truly God's Word belongs in God's Book. If a writing is really inspired so that it is true and divine, then it is canonical. Inspiration is the test of canonicity. Of course, we are not through yet. We have to get a good test of the inspiration of a book.

This concept also explains some other things. Apparently one writer often purposely hooked his book onto the preceding one. Joshua 24:26 does not say Joshua wrote a book. It says he "wrote these words in the book of the law of God," that is, he added his section to Moses' writing. We usually think that Joshua wrote just his twenty-four chapters. But it seems more likely that Joshua's word begins with Deuteronomy 34 and ends at Joshua 24:28.

Many destructive critics have made fun of the idea that Moses wrote the Pentateuch, for, they say, how could Moses write Deuteronomy 34, the account of his own death? But they have not noticed that frequently an Old Testament book ends with something which was most probably attached by the next author. It seems that the prophets were conscious that they were writing a continued story and they often added an appendix on the previous author's work to tie their own in more closely to what preceded. Thus Joshua would have added the account of Moses' death (Deut. 34). The author of Judges would have added the record of Joshua's death (Josh. 24:29-33), part of which is identical with Judges 2:7-9. Samuel would have added to Judges-Ruth the genealogy of David found in Ruth 4:17-22. The clearest case of this is the last two verses of II Chronicles which are identical with the first three verses of Ezra. This would have been strange if the prophets had each been writing for themselves. But it seems perfectly natural if we remember that each prophet was writing his additional section to the book of God's revelation.

The best illustration of this continuity is the books of Samuel and Kings. These books cover from 1050 to 560 B.C. Very likely they were written by a succession of prophets from Samuel on down. The first two books bear the name of Samuel, but Samuel's death occurs in I Samuel 25:1. They really are a history of David. We know that the histories of the kings of Israel and Judah were written by a succession of prophets. I and II Chronicles refer to such histories as source books for their own histories. They say that the story of David was written by Samuel, Nathan, and Gad (I Chron. 29:29); the history of Solomon by Nathan, Ahijah, and Iddo (II Chron. 9:29); that of Rehoboam by Shemaiah and Iddo (II Chron. 12:15); of Abijah by Iddo (II Chron. 13:22); of Jehoshaphat by Jehu the son of Hanani (II Chron. 20:34); of Uzziah and Hezekiah by Isaiah (II Chron. 26:22; 32:32). Furthermore, it seems plain from a comparison of Samuel-Kings with Chronicles that Chronicles' main source book for its history was in fact Samuel-Kings. It follows, therefore, that Samuel-Kings essentially is this continued history of the kings of Israel and Judah, written by these prophets over a space of four hundred years.

We might ask, How did Samuel-Kings get in the canon? The answer is that in those days everybody knew it was written by these accredited spokesmen for God. How did they know these men were accredited of God? They showed the same sort of miracles and their predictions were fulfilled in the same way as was true of Moses. Many of these miracles and predictions are recorded. Many doubtless are omitted. But the believing people of Israel could easily tell who were prophets of God, and their books would naturally be accepted in the canon. The books of Samuel-Kings have always been classified among the prophets by the Jews and are also so classified in the New Testament.

There were other great prophets. Some of these wrote not histories, but books of sermons and instructions. Isaiah wrote both his own book and a part of the history. You may have noticed that II Kings 19 is identical with Isaiah 37. Ezekiel, Daniel, Hosea, Joel, and other minor prophets also added their books to the canon.

We have cases where one book quotes another as canonical. We have mentioned Samuel-Kings and Chronicles. II Chronicles 36:21 also quotes Jeremiah 25:11 as authoritative. Daniel 9:2 quotes the same passage of Jeremiah as being in one of "the books" (ASV) which give "the word of the Lord." Similarly, Jeremiah 26:18 quotes Micah 3:12 as a prophecy. There are many other quotations and cross references which show that these books were accepted as true and canonical by their contemporaries.

Now a word about the remaining books of the Old Testament. Were the Psalms canonical? Of course they were. Most of them were clearly written by prophets. David himself wrote about half and he was a prophet (Acts 2:30). Heman, Jeduthun, and Asaph are called prophets in I Chronicles 25:1-5.

How about Proverbs, Song of Solomon and Ecclesiastes? These books seem clearly to have been written by Solomon.

Was Solomon a prophet? We sometimes are hard on Solomon because his foreign wives eventually led him astray into idolatry. It seems that as an important king he made many treaties with surrounding nations and cities. In ancient days, treaties were sealed with a political marriage. The bride was often little more than a hostage. But Solomon thought he had to treat these wives with respect as some of their fathers were powerful rulers. So finally he compromised his faith and built them idol sanctuaries as they requested. But at the beginning, Solomon was true to the Lord and the Lord spoke to him in dreams and visions as He did to the other prophets. Nehemiah 13:26 gives Solomon his due. There is nothing wrong in seeing in him the prophetic author of Proverbs, Song of Solomon, and Ecclesiastes.

For Esther, Job, Ezra, and Chronicles our evidence is incomplete. We do know, however, that all these books were classed among the prophets by Christ and the apostles. The Jewish historian Josephus, who wrote about A.D. 90 classed them all as prophetic except Job.

## PROOF FOR OLD TESTAMENT CANON

Destructive critics have denied much of the above conclusions. They say that the Pentateuch was canonized about 400 B.C.; the books classed as Prophets in the Hebrew Bible were canonized about 200 B.C., and the miscellaneous Writings were not fully canonized until a council held in A.D. 90. They think that no books were written to be canonical, but that the Jews first loved certain books, then venerated them, and finally canonized them. But we know from the Dead Sea Scrolls that the books were canonized earlier than critics have thought.

The Dead Sea Scrolls come from around 225 B.C.-A.D. 70. So far they include copies of every Old Testament book except Esther. They also include other books dealing with special

Essene beliefs and some of the apocryphal books. Only the Old Testament books were considered authoritative.

The Essene writings quote from and refer to the Pentateuch, Isaiah, Ezekiel, Zechariah, Psalms, Daniel, Proverbs, and many others as fully authoritative and canonical. One of the main contributions of the Dead Sea Scrolls, though sometimes it is unnoticed, is this early witness to our Old Testament canon.

The fact is that the destructive critics were building their theories on the order of the Old Testament books in our present Hebrew Bibles. The present day Hebrew Bibles have three divisions—the Law with five books, the Prophets with eight books, and the miscellaneous Writings with eleven books. This makes twenty-four which, because of combining some, equals our thirty-nine. This division of the books can be traced back to the Jewish Talmud of about A.D. 400. But critics forget that much happened in Jewry before the Talmud. And the earlier listings do not support the Talmudic division.

As mentioned before, Josephus in A.D. 90 lists twenty-two books. (He attached Ruth to Judges and Lamentations to Jeremiah, as many early authors did. It adds up to our thirty-nine.) He has five books in the Law, thirteen in the Prophets, and four in the Writings. He calls the third division "hymns to God and precepts for the conduct of human life." It probably included Psalms, Job, Proverbs, and Ecclesiastes. The critics have repeatedly said that Daniel was not written until 165 B.C. and that is why it was not put in the second division of the Prophets, which included those books accepted before 200 B.C. But this sounds passing strange. Josephus says Daniel *was* among the prophets in his day. And we have about six copies of Daniel among the Dead Sea Scrolls, the earliest of which is dated 110 B.C. And it was recognized as Scripture. The old critical theory of three stages of canonization just does not fit the facts.

There are two points of evidence for a threefold canon earlier than Josephus, but neither one lists which books are in each section. Luke 24:44 speaks of the Law and the Prophets and the Psalms. The prologue to the apocryphal book of Ecclesiasticus in 130 B.C. speaks of the Law, Prophets, and other books of the fathers. Just as early, however, are the witnesses for a twofold division which was later subdivided. The New Testament a dozen times refers to Moses and the Prophets, or the Law and the Prophets, etc. And the Dead Sea Manual of Discipline and the Zadokite Fragments, also in the Dead Sea literature, four times refer to the sacred writings as the "Law and the Prophets," or a similar title. The Septuagint—the Greek translation of the Old Testament done about 200 B.C.—also evidences this twofold division. All the evidence points to this conclusion. The law was written by the great prophet Moses. The books of the following prophets were also accepted as of equal authority and their writings were put in a second division as they were written one by one.

Certain it is that our Old Testament books were the ones received by Jesus and the apostles, and for Christians this would seem to settle the matter. The books received by the Jews of Jesus' day were clearly our thirty-nine books. The New Testament quotes from nearly all the thirty-nine books. It does not quote from the apocrypha.

The fourteen apocryphal books were not officially recognized by the Roman Catholic Church until A.D. 1545. They were not accepted by Jerome, who made the Latin translation which Catholics use today. The Apocryphal books do not claim to be the Word of God nor the work of prophets. While they are interesting and valuable as history, they are not Scripture. As Hebrews 1:1 puts it: "God . . . spake . . . by the prophets."

## The New Testament Canon

The study of the New Testament canon is in some respects easier than that of the Old. To begin with, all branches of Christendom, the Protestant, Roman Catholic, Greek Orthodox, agree on our twenty-seven New Testament books. In the New Testament field, the questions do not come so much from those who ask which books are inspired, as from those who doubt if any books are inspired, that is, from liberals of all shades. Again, the Protestant test of canonicity is inspiration, but unfortunately the question is about inspiration itself. Officially, all Christians are agreed on our New Testament. But actually, the Roman Catholics overlay it with the traditions of Mariolatry, etc., and the liberal and Neo-orthodox Protestants deny its full truthfulness. So again we should be informed on New Testament questions.

Fortunately, much information is available. The New Testament was not written in the dim light of a strange background, but in the height of Greco-Roman culture, and much of the history of that day has come down across the centuries to us.

Many Christians are not aware that we have a good bit of writing from the early Christian church beside the New Testament. The New Testament, being the Word of God, occupies us so fully that we sometimes forget we have a number of Christian classics written by men who lived during and immediately after the apostles' time, and who in some cases gave their lives for their faith. These Christian classics should be read by more people. Much more interesting than early secular literature, they breathe a spirit of true Christian devotion and enable us more fully to appreciate our faith. Nearly all are found in the series of books called "Ante-Nicene Fathers." Why not look them up in some library and read them for yourself—especially the first volume.

Our study of the New Testament canon will start at a time when the acceptance of the New Testament books is fairly clear and complete, and work backward to the earliest days when our evidence just begins. Then we shall see what the New Testament itself teaches, which, after all, is final for the Christian.

Our first stage of study will be around A.D. 170. After this time there were dozens of writers on the subject of canonicity, and the agreement on the canon was well-nigh unanimous, except for flash backs and special controversies.

First to be considered is the Muratorian Canon. This is a copy of a document written about 170. It is a listing of the books that were accepted as New Testament Scripture in the Christian church—books which were allowed to be read publicly, i.e., in church services. For us it is just what we are looking for. The beginning of the writing is broken, but it evidently spoke of Matthew and Mark, for it calls Luke the author of the "third" Gospel and says "Paul had associated him with himself." John's Gospel is listed and I John 1:1 is also quoted. It adds that the same "principal Spirit" speaks in all the Gospels. Next it mentions Acts by Luke and then thirteen epistles written, it says, by Paul. It warns against some forged letters. Then are mentioned the epistle of Jude and two of John (some think II and III John were joined) and finally the Revelation of John. Also it says, "We receive the Apocalypse of Peter," though it admits that some do not. Today we know that it was a forgery. It adds that we cannot accept the Shepherd of Hermas because it was written recently and cannot be placed "among the apostles to the end of time."

This is a very good list. It excludes all the forgeries but one, and includes all our canonical books except Hebrews, James, and the two epistles of Peter. Westcott, who has written carefully on this subject, thinks that the present document was copied from a manuscript that had a break here, for we know that other contemporary sources mention these four books.

Irenaeus is another witness of this period. He has left extensive writings, which fortunately have been preserved. His chief work was a five-volume treatise against the heresies of his day. The main heresy was Gnosticism, which literally means being "in the know." But unfortunately those who claim to be in the know are often in the dark. These Gnostics attached the Christian teaching to Greek philosophy and other speculation which pictured God as a distant immovable force who operated through a host of lesser deities like Jesus Christ, and Chaos, and Jehovah, and Silence, and other principalities and powers.

Irenaeus dealt with Gnosticism in a careful and scholarly manner, refuting it by both common sense and Scripture. Irenaeus' writings give the feeling that one is in touch with a capable, earnest Christian student. And surely Irenaeus emphasizes both the Old Testament and the New. He speaks of it just as we would, the Word of God, the truth, the writings of the prophets and apostles, the Scriptures. He refutes heresy, using each of the four Gospels extensively; then uses Acts and the "apostolical epistles." He does a thorough job. His admiration for the apostles, including Paul, is unbounded.

Specifically he quotes from all the New Testament books except Philemon and III John. He names most of the books and discusses their authorship. He declares that the Apostle John wrote the Gospel, I and II John and the Revelation. The latter he dates at about A.D. 95. He says Peter wrote I Peter. He does not specifically give the author of I and II Timothy, Titus, Hebrews, James, II Peter, and Jude, but he definitely quotes all these, though he touches on Hebrews only once or twice. Once he seems to attribute this book to Paul. He denounces the Gospel of Thomas as a forgery and the Gospel of Truth as non-apostolic. Surely his lack of quotation from Philemon and III John is attributable to the fact that these short epistles did not contain material pertinent to his argument against Gnosticism. He possessed and revered our New Testament.

An earlier stage of importance is around A.D. 140. The great names here are Justin Martyr and, in light of recent discoveries, the heretic Valentinus. There were other authors of the time, but they only confirm these two, and for brevity's sake they must be omitted. Justin was born around 100 and reared near Shechem in Palestine. He was very much interested in philosophy, but in his seeking he found more problems than answers. One philosopher after a short time asked for his tuition fee so that the instruction would be profitable to both teacher and student! Justin figured this was good business but poor philosophy, and quit. Finally he received a Christian testimony from an old man who directed him, as Westcott says, "from Plato to the Prophets, from metaphysics to faith." Three books by Justin are still available. A number of his writings are lost. He wrote around 145-148 and died a martyr's death.

Justin leaves us a witness to only ten of the New Testament books, but his attitude toward these is important. Especially vital is his very frequent reference to the Gospels. All four are used and treated as Scripture. He calls them "memoirs of the apostles and those who followed them," showing that he knew the details of the writing of Mark and Luke. Once he refers to the Apostle Peter and to something "written in his memoirs," proceeding to refer to an incident from Mark. He clearly considered Mark as the recorder of Peter's preaching.

Justin is of special interest as he gives us our earliest description of a church service. He says the people gather on a Sunday, the Prophets and the "memoirs of the apostles" are read, the president explains them and exhorts; this is followed by the taking of bread and wine, and finally the collection. Not a bad Protestant church service—even the collection! The special significance is in the obvious equation of Old and New Testament Scriptures for reading in the church. Also vital is his testimony to Revelation as from the pen of John. The epistles he refers to are Romans, Corinthians, Colossians, II Thessalonians, and Hebrews.

We should add here the witness of a lesser known man of Egypt, Pantaenus. Like Polycarp, whom we shall meet later, he lived to a great age. We have nothing from him, but his disciple Clement of Alexandria indicates that he held the Pauline authorship of Hebrews. This witness in Egypt is as early as Justin's in Rome.

Among the heretical teachings of Gnosticism, those of Valentinus and Basilides stand out. Basilides lived some years earlier than Justin, perhaps around A.D. 125. Nothing of his works remain except quotations by others. Still we are told he acknowledged Matthew, Luke, John, Romans, I and II Corinthians, I Timothy and I Peter. He is the first author definitely to quote these books as Scripture.

Basilides' later contemporary Valentinus was an Egyptian who moved to Rome. Tertullian, of about A.D. 200, says Valentinus, unlike some heretics, accepted the whole Scripture. He wrote a so-called Gospel of Truth which Irenaeus roundly condemns but which was lost for centuries. This work has recently been found in Egypt and was published in 1956. It is, as Irenaeus said, a heretical Gnostic treatise and yet, as Tertullian testified, it shows that Valentinus used almost all our New Testament books. Even Hebrews and Revelation are included. It seems clear that at Rome in 140 they had our New Testament.

WITNESS OF THREE ANCIENT WORTHIES

We take another leap backward, omitting some lesser men, and come to the first generation after the apostles—indeed the later contemporaries of the apostles. Clement of Rome

wrote a letter to the Corinthians about A.D. 95, actually about
the same time John wrote Revelation. Ignatius of Antioch
wrote seven letters on his way to martyrdom in Rome about
107. Polycarp, who lived on to old age, wrote a letter to the
Philippian church about 108. Let us put together the witness of these three ancient worthies. Their writings are not
extensive, but they are rich. Together they witness to all the
New Testament books except Luke, Colossians, II and
III John, Jude and Revelation. Clement declares that the
apostles were sent by Christ to preach. He likens their foreknowledge of church troubles to Moses' foreknowledge. He
reminds the Corinthians of the epistle written to them by
"the blessed apostle Paul" "under the inspiration of the
Spirit." This was the attitude of a leader of the church while
the last apostle was still alive.

Ignatius, in his letter to the Ephesians, refers by name to
their letter from "Paul the holy, the martyred." In writing
to the Philadelphian church he mentions the "gospel and
apostles" in terms equal to those used for the prophets of the
Old Testament. This, be it noted, was the name early used
for the New Testament.

Polycarp is the most interesting of the three, for he lived to
a great age in Ephesus and knew the Apostle John well. He
died a martyr's death about 155. Irenaeus knew Polycarp
and thus was himself only once removed from the Apostle
John. Polycarp's short epistle to the Philippians is filled with
references to the New Testament writings. Acts, ten epistles
of Paul, I John, I Peter, and possibly II Peter are used. He
refers by name to the epistle to the Philippians written by
the "blessed and glorified Paul" who had "accurately and
steadfastly taught the word of truth" to them. Apparently
in chapter 12 he quotes Ephesians 4:26 as Scripture. Alto-
gether Polycarp is a worthy representative of the earliest
church which learned straight from the apostles themselves.

## WHAT NEW TESTAMENT BOOKS SAY ABOUT EACH OTHER

We now take another jump of only a few years right back into New Testament times. What do the New Testament books say about each other? What do they claim for themselves?

The clearest reference in any book to another is found in II Peter 3:15, 16. Here Peter recommends Paul's epistles—all his epistles—and expressly calls them Scripture. This is an extremely valuable witness. The attitude of the early church toward the Old Testament Scriptures is clear. They were inspired, true, authoritative, canonical. To put Paul's epistles on a par with these was to give them the highest regard possible. Notice, Peter does not consider merely certain books of Paul to be inspired. It is not that only Romans and Ephesians are Scripture. No, to Peter everything that Paul wrote is Scripture. We could not want more specific testimony.

Paul likewise quotes Luke. In I Corinthians 9:9 Paul takes up the question of salary for ministers and argues rather neatly from Moses' Law on the caring for an ox threshing grain. He draws out the argument to some length. In I Timothy 5:18 he returns to this subject. But this time his appeal to Moses' Law is quite brief: "For the scripture saith, Thou shalt not muzzle the ox that treadeth out the corn." This time, however, he adds, "And the labourer is worthy of his reward." He settles the whole question quickly and briefly by quoting Luke 10:7 (the words are identical in the Greek). But notice Luke is paralleled with Deuteronomy as "Scripture."

The third case is Jude 18 which quotes II Peter 3:3. Jude quotes it as authoritative and declares it is a word from the apostles. The value of this last instance is great, for II Peter has less evidence in its favor from early Christian authors. It is providential that it has this positive support from within the New Testament itself. Actually, these three brief instances witness to the early acceptance as Scripture of a Gospel, Paul's epistles, and one of the general epistles. This is broad support.

## WHAT NEW TESTAMENT BOOKS CLAIM FOR THEMSELVES

The claims the books make for themselves is a bigger subject. It is essential first to note that the books do clearly claim authority. These are not accidental writings which someone fondly collected later, as a biographer might collect George Washington's "Letters." If that were the case, we might question the New Testament. Most of us have written some letters we would rather not see in a collection! But these writings were done on purpose and were given by the apostles as authoritative.

The second epistle Paul wrote was II Thessalonians. In it he says, "If any man obey not our word by this epistle, note that man, and have no company with him" (II Thess. 3:14). This is strong language—to excommunicate a man who disobeys his epistle. But II Thessalonians 2:15 says the same thing. From II Thessalonians 3:17 we may conclude that Paul decided to guard his letters against forgery in view of false epistles that were being circulated (II Thess. 2:2). He decided to conclude his epistles always the same way, perhaps also to sign them. Every Pauline epistle after this—including Hebrews—concludes with similar words. Romans has the characteristic ending at the conclusion of chapter 15, as chapter 16 seems to be a postscript of personal greetings.

Colossians 4:16 directs that this epistle and the epistle of Laodicea be read publicly in the two churches. We remember that public reading was in the early church the mark of canonical books. In the synagogues the Jews read the Old Testament Scriptures every Sabbath, and in the same way in the church the prophets and apostles were read publicly. Paul was directing that his epistles be received as canonical.

Some have worried about the epistle of the Laodiceans. It is possible that in early persecutions this letter was lost. After all, only a few of the words of Christ are preserved and most of the oral sermons of the apostles are lost. But it is also quite likely that this lost epistle is actually the Ephesian epistle. The best manuscripts of Ephesians 1:1 do not include the words "which are at Ephesus." It was perhaps a general letter sent to both Ephesus and near-by Laodicea.

Some allege another lost letter is referred to in I Corinthians 5:9. But this is probably only an "epistolary aorist" as the Greek grammarians say. It means that this is what he wrote just above in this epistle. Ephesians 3:3 is another such reference.

In I Corinthians 14:37 Paul declares that his writings are "the commandments of the Lord," and a spiritual man would know it. The claim here is quite emphatic. Indeed it is so positive that we should be able to drop the matter except that some argue the opposite from I Corinthians 7:12. They say that Paul sometimes gave the Lord's word, sometimes his own. This would be a strange interpretation, for it would make Paul contradict himself in the same book. The true interpretation, clearly, is that Paul is referring here as elsewhere to quotations from Jesus Christ during His earthly ministry. Paul quoted Christ's words against divorce, but on the problem of mixed marriages, the Lord had not directly spoken. On this, Paul gave his own word—which itself was given by the Holy Spirit as he indicates with some fine sarcasm, in verse 40.

Several of the other New Testament books also make similar claims. But all do not. They did not all need to. John practically signs his name to the fourth Gospel (John 21:24). Luke and Acts were written to Theophilus, who of course knew all the details of the writing. As the books were circulated, likely the details were circulated too. Early authors like Justin Martyr inform us that Luke wrote these books for Paul. Papias, of A.D. 140, and others say that Mark wrote the second Gospel as a helper of Peter, writing down his teaching. We have the names of two such secretaries given in Romans 16:22 and I Peter 5:12. Sometimes the apostles used such helpers, sometimes not. Many think that Paul's eyesight was poor and it was difficult for him to write for himself (Gal. 6:11 is sometimes translated "with how large letters I have written unto you with my own hand"). In any case, all four Gospels were received by the early church as apostolic, inspired and canonical. Paul himself, as we have just shown, quoted the third Gospel as Scripture.

Perhaps the best example of the claims of a New Testament book is found in Revelation 22:18, 19. These verses have a most solemn curse for anyone who would dare to change the words of this book of Scripture. In principle the words apply to the whole Bible. These books are canonical, they are the truth of God, inspired by God's Spirit whom Christ had promised in special measure to the apostles (John 14:26; 16:13; 20:22).

We have argued that the books of the New Testament are apostolic and inspired. They were written during the first century and accepted at once by the early church as authoritative. Happily, there is a tendency recently to accept much of this conclusion. Newly discovered documents, especially writings of early Gnostics, have supported these conclusions. Gnosticism of the second century is clearly a later thing than the teachings given in the canonical Scriptures.

Whereas destructive critics of a generation ago declared that some parts of the New Testament were not written until A.D. 170, the tendency now is for even critics to say that it was all finished within the first century and mostly before A.D. 80. This is a great advance in study of the canon. It means that our New Testament was written by the apostles and canonized under their supervision. Also, we must insist, it was believed and accepted by that generation that had seen Jesus' works and lived beside the empty tomb. The church did not create the New Testament, as Roman Catholics say. The apostles, under God, created the New Testament, and the Holy Spirit using the apostles and their writings created the church. The church was founded by God upon the truth of Christ. That truth is enshrined and preserved in the New Testament.

*Chapter 5*

# WERE THE OLD TESTAMENT PROPHECIES REALLY PROPHETIC?

*by*

ROBERT D. CULVER

*Chapter 5*

# WERE THE OLD TESTAMENT PROPHECIES REALLY PROPHETIC?

WHEN THE EARLY CHRISTIANS began to preach they declared vigorously that God had acted in history through the appearance, ministry, and atoning death of His Son, Jesus of Nazareth,[1] to obtain forgiveness of all sins and sure hope of eternal life with God. The New Testament record reports that they never failed to support these remarkable claims with proof that the claims were true. They declared the significance they assigned to Jesus was proved true by His miraculous resurrection from the dead and by the fact that the events which transpired in connection with His life and death had been supernaturally predicted by the Old Testament.[2] They further claimed that their own eyes had seen these things occur and that their testimony was true.[3] Such proof they held to be sufficient for them to command men to acknowledge Jesus Christ as Lord.[4] These proofs produced such assurance in the apostles themselves that they risked their lives for the sake of the Gospel; and the same sort of assurance prevailed in their followers.

The first Christian sermon is an example of the apostles' confident authority. "Jesus of Nazareth . . . ye have taken,

[1]Acts 2:22, 23, 37-40; 3:12-15, 19; 10:34-43; 13:22-30; 17:30, 31.
[2]Acts 2:23-26; 3:15-18; 10:40-43; 13:29-37; 17:30, 31.
[3]Acts 2:32; 3:15; 4:20; 10:39-41; 13:31; 17:30, 31.
[4]Acts 2:36, 38; 3:19; 4:10-12, 20; 7:51-53; 13:38-52; 17:30, 31.

and by wicked hands have crucified and slain: whom God raised up" (Acts 2:22-24)—the miraculous resurrection of Jesus. "This is that which was spoken by the prophet Joel . . . David speaketh concerning him. . . . Therefore being a prophet, and knowing that God had sworn with an oath to him, that of the fruit of his loins, according to the flesh, he would raise up Christ to sit on his throne; he seeing this before spake of the resurrection of Christ" (Acts 2:16, 25, 30, 31)—this is citation of fulfilled prophecy as proof. "This Jesus hath God raised up, whereof we all are witnesses" (Acts 2:32)—this is the claim to be eyewitnesses of the events reported.

This is the New Testament "proof" of the truthfulness of Christianity. The same approach is taken repeatedly in the New Testament. In following this line of proof the apostles were doing only that which had been done by God's prophets for centuries. Before we turn to specific Old Testament prophecies, however, observe that we are doing far more than discovering the Bible's approach, important as that is. We are actually examining the testimony of God to His written Word and discovering *why* we must believe what the Bible says.[5]

### *How the Bible Uses the Evidence of Fulfilled Prophecy*

First of all let us see how the fulfillment of divine prophey gave assurance to the patriarchs. Abraham was told that he and his wife would have a son through whom God's many promises to the family (Gen. 12:1-3; 15:14-16) would be fulfilled. When faith was failing, Sarah being in her ninetieth year and Abraham in his hundredth, God promised them a son within the next year (Gen. 18:11-14). Though the faith of the mother was weak (Gen. 18:10-12), within a

[5]See Exodus 6:7; 10:1, 2; 5:15, 18; 14:31; 16:6, 12; 18:11; 34:10; Numbers 4:11; 14:22; 16:28; Deuteronomy 29:2 ff.; 34:10-12; I Kings 8:59, 60; 18:36, 37; Psalms 77; 105; Isaiah 41:21-24; 45:9, 10, 20-25; 46:9, 10.

year the child was born (Gen. 21:1, 2). Sarah had laughed
in her doubt (Gen. 18:12), and as if to rebuke that incipient
unbelief, Abraham named the baby "Laughter," for such is
the meaning of Isaac. This fulfillment of prophecy in such
a remarkable way brought strong assurance to the parents.

Similar experiences were granted to Jacob and especially
to Joseph, but we pass on to the remarkable fulfillments of
prophecy for the assurance of Moses.

We think of Moses as a staunch believer and a veritable
giant in leadership. But he was not always that way. When
God first found him he was weak-kneed and vacillating
(Exod. 3:11; 4:1, 10). Fulfillment of divine prophecy was
important in bringing about the change. He was told that
the very place on which he then stood would later be a
place where he and the Israelites would worship God, the
Mount of God, also called Horeb and Sinai (Exod. 3:11, 12).
This is precisely what happened, as Exodus 19:1—40:38 reports.

Furthermore, God predicted to the recalcitrant Moses that
his brother Aaron was at that moment already on his way
to meet him (Exod. 4:14), that they would soon have a joy-
ful meeting after forty years of separation, and that they
would have their meeting also at the hallowed scene of the
burning bush, the Mount of God. This too came to pass
(Exod. 4:27, 28). These experiences were only the beginning of the strong assurance God gave to Moses by prophecy
and its fulfillment. The rest was to come to him and the
Israelites that they all might believe God and that Moses'
authority might be highly regarded.

In one sense the ten plagues of Egypt and the remarkable
dividing of the waters of the Red Sea following were marvels
of God's power. In another sense every one of them was a
miracle of divine omniscience, the fulfillment of a prophecy
made by God's appointed messenger and announced by
him in connection with his claims to speak for God. This

was "apologetics" indeed! Moses and Aaron would stand in the presence of Pharaoh and declare that the waters of Egypt were to become blood (Exod. 7:17), and the waters were changed. Or they would announce a plague of frogs (Exod. 8:1-3), and the frogs came. Then they might foretell the end of the plague on the morrow (Exod. 8:9-13). Sometimes the details involved were quite remarkable, as for instance, that certain of the plagues would affect the Egyptians only, not the Hebrews. When this marvelous series of divine manifestations was over, climaxed by the crossing of the Red Sea between the walls of water (Exod. 7-14) just as Moses had predicted, there was not a man of Israel who did not know in his heart of hearts (Exod. 14:30, 31) that Jehovah was God and that Moses was His servant. This, of course, was exactly what these events were designed by God to accomplish.

Forty years later, when poised for the attack on Canaan, Moses was about to die. The new civil and military leader, Joshua, had already been selected. But there was no one yet to take Moses' place as God's messenger. At this juncture the office of prophet, with a succession of men to fill it, was announced (Deut. 18:9-18). The several qualifications of the prophet need not concern us here with one exception. There was possibility of impostors. One of the means by which the impostor might be infallibly detected was his ability to predict the future (Deut. 18:21, 22). These predictions were not to be long-range prophecies of the remote future but short-range ones that could be observed and tested by the people of the prophet's own time.

Elijah is a case of a prophet who preached but did not produce Scripture. Like a bolt from the blue he appears on the pages of Scripture at I Kings 17:1; saying to Ahab, "As the Lord God of Israel liveth, before whom I stand, there shall not be dew nor rain these years, but according to my word." Elijah was going to have some things to say concerning eternal truth, but in the meantime he was laying the groundwork of his authority as a prophet. When three years later, after the miracle of fire in the contest with Baal's prophets on Mount Carmel, the rain came again exactly when he said it would, then the Israelites could not doubt that the LORD was God and Elijah His prophet (I Kings 18:36-38, 41-46).

The last great prophet, the consummation of the line of the prophets, was our Lord Himself. There were others in the apostolic age who spoke by special divine revelation, but all these spoke by His authority and were but channels of His revelation. When Jesus came, He too was certified as a true messenger of God in the same way. The Jews asked for a sign of His authority, and He predicted His resurrection (Matt. 12:38-40; John 2:13-22). When John the Baptist wanted a sign that the Messiah stood before him, God let him know ahead of time that in some visible manner he would see the Spirit of God descending on the Messiah (John 1:33). When at Jesus' baptism John saw exactly that, fulfilled prophecy had again given its seal of certainty (John 1:29-32). When later John from his cell in jail asked for further assurance, Jesus only alluded to His fulfillment of ancient prophecies (Matt. 11:2-6; cf. Isa. 29:18; 35:5, 6; 61:1).

The most extensive evidential use of fulfilled prophecy in the Bible itself is in the portion of Isaiah which begins with chapter 40 and leads up to the marvelous prediction of our Lord's career in chapter 53. In this section the Lord God Himself is represented in contest with the impotent gods of paganism for the minds of men. The theme running through the passage, in part, is that the Lord alone is God for He alone can act. Among His mightiest acts is true prediction of the future. The entire section should be read at this point, but let us extract a few verses.

"Produce your cause, saith the LORD; bring forth your

strong reasons, saith the King of Jacob. Let them bring them forth, and show us what shall happen: let them show the former things, what they be, that we may consider them, and know the latter end of them; or declare us things for to come. Show us the things that are to come hereafter, that we may know that ye are gods: yea, do good, or do evil, that we may be dismayed, and behold it together. Behold, ye are of nothing, and your work of nought: an abomination is he that chooseth you" (Isa. 41:21-24). In this manner God demonstrates His magnificient solitary grandeur, showing that He alone is God—for He alone can either reconstruct the unknown or forgotten past, or predict the unknown future. In the same tenor, but even more emphatically, the Lord later says: "I am God, and there is none else; I am God, and there is none like me, declaring the end from the beginning, and from ancient times the things that are not yet done" (Isa. 46:9, 10).

Thus we have seen that from the very earliest times in the history of revelation and redemption the fulfillment of prophecy has been a strong proof of the validity of God's own claims and the claims of His messengers. This has been observed in the assurance of the pre-Mosaic patriarchs, in the accreditation of Moses to the Israelites, in the support of the faith given to the Hebrews at the time of the exodus, and from thence onward to New Testament times. Messiah Himself and God His Father have placed their confidence in this mode of apologetical proof.

### *Validity of Apologetical Use of Fulfilled Prophecy*

Fulfilled prophecy, however, is only part of the base of Biblical evidences. In fact, standing alone it would prove nothing except that some men in the history of the world have had a strange, inexplicable knowledge of the future. It is the connection of this supernatural power with the miracles of Scripture (i.e., those reported and authorized therein), the relation of both miracles and prophecy with the Jewish people and the claims of their prophets, apostles, and Messiah, that makes the case for Christianity an infallible one.

Even so it must be remembered that though God has declared the case a certain one, it is possible for men to deny it (Isa. 53:1-3; cf. John 12:37-41; Acts 3:1-4:22, especially 4:13-18; Acts 17:30-32). The Gospel will always remain foolishness to the minds of sinful men until the Holy Spirit enlightens them (I Cor. 1:18; 2:14). The important thing for us to see in this connection is that if men fail at this point, the root of the failure is not in their *mental* faculties but in their *spiritual* ones; that their rejection is not based on *intellectual* obstacles but on *moral* ones. Their arguments prove that they are vital and active mentally, but as to spiritual things "dead in trespasses and sins" (Eph. 2:1-3; cf. I Cor. 2:14).

Sometimes men simply reject fulfillment of prophecy as impossible and without bringing the "case to court" refuse to examine the evidence. When the evidence is thrust upon them, various expedients are devised. In the case of people who endorse outright materialism or atheism, we must seek to convince them of the existence of a personal, transcendent Creator-God. Until this is done they will not even consider the evidence. And yet it must be admitted that the only conclusive proof of the existence of the Christian God is in the miraculous deeds by which He has borne witness to Himself. The nature of the situation requires supernatural acts as proof. This, to use a technical phrase, is to say that the rational arguments of natural theology are useful in that they may remove philosophical objections to the true Christian evidences. Fortunately most people will at least consider the evidence. The average citizen, however this-worldly his interests, does not find it difficult to accept the possibility of the supernatural.

The common device for voiding the evidential value of Biblical prophecies appears to have been invented in the third Christian century by a pagan philosopher named Porphyry (A.D. 233-304). This man was the most noted disciple of Plotinus, the father of the movement known as Neoplatonism, a system of thought which taught that the universe emanates out of God and that salvation is achieved by ascetic practices. St. Augustine reports that Porphyry was brought up a Christian and after becoming apostate wrote against Christianity from a spirit of revenge.[6] A very clever writer, Porphyry saw that if he could convince men that the predictions of the Old Testament, especially the detailed ones of the book of Daniel, were written after the events they predict had transpired, then he would have destroyed one of the main supports for their faith in the inspiration of Scripture and in Christianity.[7] Little has been added to Porphyry's arguments (so far as they are known), though his method has become exceedingly popular among liberal higher critics.

It is not possible to discover very much outside the Bible itself to show exactly when these prophecies were written. Happily some of the most striking ones were written at a time (even according to the claims and admissions of unbelieving critics) long before the events they predict took place. If we can discover in the case of only these that true miraculous prediction of the future took place, then we have strong proof of the supernatural origin of the Bible and support for faith that the claims of Scripture as to date and authorship of its various portions are true. All the predictions then may be introduced as valid evidence.

[6]*The City of God,* Book X, Section 20.
[7]Porphyry's arguments are reported by Jerome (fourth century A.D.) in his *Commentary on Daniel* recently translated by Gleason L. Archer, Jr., and published by Baker Book House. See especially the Prologue, pp. 15-18.

### *Essential Features of Predictive Prophecy*

It must be recognized that prophecies of the sort under consideration will have some distinctive characteristics. They will not be mere sage remarks, or scientific prediction based on laws of nature. Neither will they reflect a humanly controlled situation wherein the prophet or his supporters fulfill the prophecy. They must be predictions of the future such as only God could know and bring to pass.

Another necessary feature is a degree of obscurity in many of the predictions. At first thought this might seem seriously to weaken the evidential value. Actually it is the basis of its strength. The prophecy ordinarily will have a true but obscure reference to future events.

Jesus' predictions of His resurrection will serve as typical examples. In His prophecy of Matthew 12:40 He did not clearly say He would die, that His body would be buried, and that three days later His body would be resurrected, leaving a tomb empty. Rather He made an enigmatical reference to Jonah's experience in the "whale" and indicated that He would have a similar experience in the "heart of the earth," i.e., underground. When He predicted the resurrection in connection with His cleansing of the temple (John 2:18, 19), He said, "Destroy this temple, and in three days I will raise it up." Actually, except for Jesus Himself, no one on earth really understood those predictions until after the resurrection and then only with considerable reflection (John 2:20, 21). When prophecy had become history, then with reflection it was seen that our Lord was speaking of the resurrection, and that unmistakably (John 2:22). If this obscurity were not initially present, prophecy might actually produce either its nonfulfillment through the efforts of those who might wish to oppose it, or its evidential value might be destroyed by the bungling efforts of other too-helpful friends who would try to bring it to pass.

Thus, far from being a flaw in the evidence, this feature is one of the strengths of the evidence of fulfilled prophecy. It is like a case presented either by the prosecution or defense in court when a true verdict is issued at the time of decision. As the case is being assembled, the pieces may seem difficult, disconnected, and obscure. But once the truth is known, all fit a pattern. Or like a disassembled jigsaw puzzle, only dimly connected with a picture when lying in its box, it assumes an unmistakable picture pattern when once it is assembled. The full design cannot be known till the pieces are put together. So the full design of prophecy, dimly seen at first, becomes clear with fulfillment.

### *Old Testament Prophecies of Christ Fulfilled in His New Testament Career*

Without doubt the most important prophecies in the Old Testament are those which relate to the coming of Christ. Christians have always believed that the chief significance of the Old Testament lies in its prophecies of Christ. In this they are only following their Lord. After His resurrection, when, as far as His first advent was concerned, *prophecy* had become *history,* He strenuously asserted that the entire Old Testament (not just isolated texts) was prophetic of Him and that to neglect this fact was for Christians both foolish and sinful. These are His words: "O fools, and slow of heart to believe all that the prophets have spoken: ought not Christ to have suffered these things, and to enter into his glory? And beginning at Moses and all the prophets, he expounded unto them in all the scriptures [i.e., the Old Testament scriptures] the things concerning himself" (Luke 24:25-27).

It would be a mistake to read the Old Testament as merely a kind of unclassified store of specific "proof texts" to show that every detail of Christ's career was specifically foreseen by some prophet. It all is predictive of Christ, but not all in the same way. The *history* of the Old Testament shows how God was getting His own people ready for His coming. It also demonstrates how desperately they needed a Saviour. The *laws* of the Old Testament were in part to teach one segment of the human race (the Hebrews) how to live in a way that a clean youth (Jesus of Nazareth) might grow to maturity among them without the corruptions of heathenism in His own home. The *institutions* of the Old Testament religion (temple, altar, laver, priests, sacrifices, rituals) had their immediate value in the worship of Israel, but even then it was understood that they pointed to a coming one and to a coming age. The *Psalms* (hymns) also had their contemporary value for worship, but they also were prophecies of Christ, and are quoted in the New Testament as predicting Christ more than any other Old Testament book. The *prophetical books* (major and minor prophets) are in the main sermons calling the Jews back to obedience to Moses' laws.

The fact that the people needed these sermons of reproof is in itself a kind of prophetic call for a Saviour from their sins. Yet aside from this general predictive quality there are many specific and detailed predictions of Christ's person and career in the Old Testament. Many of them were recognized as messianic by the Jews before and during the time of Christ. Let us select ten passages—from a verse to a chapter in length—taking them in the order in which they appear in the Bible. It will be wise to have a Bible open to these passages as we consider them.

EXAMPLES OF PROPHECY AND FULFILLMENT

GENESIS 3:15: "And I [God] will put enmity between thee and the woman, and between thy seed and her seed; it shall bruise thy head, and thou shalt bruise his heel." This is a prophecy that some member of the human race—not an angel nor spirit—would be the agent by whom deliverance would come from the awful defeat Satan inflicted on us when

he successfully enticed Eve to disobey the Lord. Jesus our
Lord was that man. The two nativity stories (early chapters
of Matthew and Luke), the four biographies (four Gospels),
and the emphatic truth of Jesus' human nature are the report
of how this aspect of the prophecy was fulfilled.

GENESIS 12:1-3: "Now the Lord had said unto Abram . . .
I will make of thee a great nation . . . thou shalt be a blessing . . . and in thee shall all families of the earth be blessed."
At this point the Bible ceases to be a report of universal
events and becomes to its end a species of Jewish history.
These verses are the first of many prophecies that the redemption of the human race would be through a people
known as Hebrews, Israelites, or Jews. The New Testament
distinctly points out how our Saviour was truly Jewish and
publicly known as such. The superscription on the cross
proclaimed Him a Jewish king; He observed the customs and
laws of the Jews; His ancestry was traced to Abraham (Matt.
1:1-17) and He was recognized even by strangers as a Jew
(John 4:9).

GENESIS 49:10: "The scepter [symbol of an ancient ruler's
authority] shall not depart from Judah, nor a lawgiver from
between his feet, until Shiloh come; and unto him shall the
gathering of the people be." The translation can be greatly
improved, as commentaries declare, but in all feasible translations this verse turns out to be a prediction that the man of
Israel who would ultimately deliver them and would rightly be their Messiah (i.e., anointed king; messiah means
anointed) would be of the tribe of Judah among the twelve
tribes. This led to the divine choice of David from one of
the families of Judah and to the birth of Jesus into his royal
line. This is explained by Matthew (1:1, 6, 11, 20) and by
Luke (3:31). Jesus was frequently recognized as a "son"
or descendant of David (Matt. 12:23; 15:22; 21:9). The
doctrinal portions of the New Testament emphasize the importance of our Lord's relation to the house of David (Rom.

1:3; II Tim. 2:8). Christ as revelator to John identified Himself as "the offspring of David" (Rev. 22:16).

II SAMUEL 7. The serious reader ought to spend a few minutes with this entire chapter before proceeding. It is a messianic passage. David had sought to build God a "house" or temple. God instructed him that quite to the contrary He, God, was about to build David a "house," not an edifice such as David had already constructed for himself, but a dynasty or line of descendants. Some of them might sin grievously and they would be chastised with severe judgments, yet the Davidic house would continue to reign forever.

"And when thy days be fulfilled . . . I will set up thy seed after thee . . . and I will establish the throne of his kingdom for ever . . . If he commit iniquity, I will chasten him with the rod of men . . . but my mercy shall not depart away from him . . . and thine house and thy kingdom shall be established for ever before thee: thy throne shall be established for ever" (II Sam. 7:12-16).

When Jesus was about to be born, the angel Gabriel announced the fulfillment of this prophecy of David's dynasty in Him. "Thou . . . shalt call his name JESUS. He shall be great, and shall be called the Son of the Highest: and the Lord God shall give unto him the throne of his father David: and he shall reign over the house of Jacob for ever; and of his kingdom there shall be no end" (Luke 1:31-33). Jesus is to have no successor. No Jew today can prove that David is his ancestor. The risen Christ alone is the proper living claimant to David's throne.

PSALM 16:8-11. This is a prophecy of the resurrection of Jesus. It is so important that Peter used it in his first Christian sermon as the main scriptural proof of the truth of Christianity. It was so convincing that three thousand Jewish converts were made. The passage is quoted in full together with Peter's inspired interpretation of it in Acts 2:25-36.

There are many other prophecies of Christ in the Psalms. Most of them, however, fall into the class of typical prediction and other indirect modes. This is of great value for doctrine, but is not especially impressive to modern people as apologetics. We therefore go on to some more impressive texts.

ISAIAH 7:14 and ISAIAH 9:6, 7: "Therefore the Lord himself shall give you a sign; Behold, a virgin shall conceive, and bear a son, and shall call his name Immanuel [i.e., God with us] . . . For unto us a child is born, unto us a son is given: and the government shall be upon his shoulder: and his name shall be called Wonderful, Counsellor, The mighty God, The everlasting Father, the Prince of Peace. Of the increase of his government and peace there shall be no end, upon the throne of David, and upon his kingdom, to order it, and to establish it with judgment and with justice from henceforth even for ever. The zeal of the Lord of hosts will perform this."

Here we have the opening and closing words of a single prophetic oracle. The majority of scholars, both liberal and conservative, agree in this. Too often expositors have sought to explain one portion of the prophecy without the other. In context it is most difficult to prove that the virgin's son has any connection at all with Mary's Babe unless one continues on to the final verses of the prophecy just quoted. Then we understand that a virgin was some day to bear a very human baby whose very character would be divine. Matthew 1:21 is the New Testament commentary. The first chapters of Matthew and Luke report the fulfillment.

ISAIAH 42:1-7. Too lengthy to quote, this reads like a poetic history of the earthly life of Jesus, or perhaps it is a rhapsodic summary statement of His holy character. An obedient Slave of God, who would please God perfectly, who would live a quiet life of gentle ministry to others in constant loyalty to justice and truth, was to teach the whole world

God's truth, establishing even Gentiles in a divine covenant of salvation. The morally blind and spiritually darkened were to be the special beneficiaries of His tender love and care. The whole Gospel story together with the expansion of the Church—not to exclude the second advent of Christ— is the record of the remarkable fulfillment of this prediction.

ISAIAH 52:13-53:12. There is not one word in these fifteen verses that is not directly predictive of Christ. They apply to Him and to no other. To read them without commentary but with some knowledge of the career of Jesus in the New Testament is a most moving and convincing experience. Those who have sought to convince unbelievers throughout the Christian centuries have relied on these verses more than all other texts of prophecy put together. Only a few excerpts can be treated here.

The whole complicated story of the background of Jesus rejection by His own people is laid out with bold strokes in Isaiah 53:1: "Who has believed what we have heard? And to whom has the arm of the LORD been revealed?" (RSV). This means Jesus was to be rejected by people who "heard" enough so that they should have believed Him, especially since His deeds of divine power ("the arm of the LORD") authenticated Him as sent of God. When the generation who had the words of the prophetic Scriptures before them knew of the message of the angels at His birth, heard the sermons of John the Baptist, the seventy, the twelve apostles, Jesus, and who had even heard the demons addressing Him as the Christ—when these people rejected the Saviour they were fulfilling their own Scriptures. Paul on a certain occasion commented on this: "They that dwell at Jerusalem, and their rulers, because they knew him not, nor yet the voices of the prophets which are read every sabbath day, they have fulfilled them in condemning him" (Acts 13:27). John 12:37-43 spells out how the rejection of the words and works proclaiming Jesus to be Messiah was fulfillment of Isaiah 53:1.

The entire life of Jesus down to the early months of His ministry was predicted in Isaiah 53:2: "For he shall grow up before him as a tender plant, and as a root out of a dry ground: he hath no form nor comeliness; and when we shall see him, there is no beauty that we should desire him." This indicates that the Servant's human development in childhood would be known to God alone ("before him," i.e., God as opposed to the nation's leaders). When He was finally to come before the nation's attention He would be a mere rustic person from an obscure and unpromising corner of the land ("tender plant . . . dry ground"). He was to be rejected not only for His undesirable origin but because of the lack of any regal "comeliness" or splendid "beauty." (This verse has nothing to do with our Lord's physical characteristics.)

The fulfillment was quite exact. He did grow up out of sight at Nazareth (Luke 2:51, 52; cf. John 1:45, 46) rather than in the glare of public notice as princes are expected to grow up. And quite far from announcing Himself as a glorious monarch from a palace and soft culture and looking the part of a king, He appeared as a foot-traveling pilgrim from Galilee and looked like a carpenter, sun-browned with calloused hands and bulging biceps. These facts of Gospel history are well known.

"He is despised and rejected of men; a man of sorrows, and acquainted with grief: and we hid as it were our faces from him; he was despised, and we esteemed him not" (Isaiah 53:3). The verse needs no explanation for our present purposes and the fulfillment is too well known to require comment.

"He was oppressed, and he was afflicted, yet he opened not his mouth: he is brought as a lamb to the slaughter, and as a sheep before her shearers is dumb, so he openeth not his mouth" (Isa. 53:7). This is exceedingly minute in its specifications. The Servant would be harassed and mistreated by

His persecutors, but He would be submissive to them and utterly unprotesting.

This is exactly what took place during that last night and day of our Lord's earthly life. They came for Him as if He were a chicken thief or housebreaker (Matt. 26:47, 55; Mark 14:43, 48; Luke 22:52) and hustled Him through several trials and beatings. But He was unprotesting and submissive, so much so that He amazed not only His persecutors but multitudes of admirers since (see Matt. 26:60-63; 27:12-14; Mark 14:60, 61; 15:2, 4; Luke 23:9). Even the thieves were amazed at it (Luke 23:39-42), and the disciples never forgot it (see I Peter 2:21-25).

"By oppression and judgment he was taken away; and as for his generation, who among them considered that he was cut off out of the land of the living for the transgression of my people to whom the stroke was due?" (Isa. 53:8 A.S.V.).

From scenes of oppressive and unjust judicial proceedings the Servant was to be hurried away. The heartbreak of it all was that none of His contemporaries understood or cared that it was on account of their sins and in their place He was to die.

How swiftly events moved that night and day! After His arrest He went through at least four or five trials of a sort. There was first the mocking in the high priest's palace before the Sanhedrin (Matt. 26:57-66). Next there was a short hearing before Pilate (Matt. 27:1; 2). After that He appeared before Herod (Luke 23:7-11), and again before Pilate (Luke 23:12-25). But neither Pilate the Roman, Herod the Edomite, nor any of the Jews "considered." Even the disciples did not understand until some weeks later.

Isaiah 53:9: "And there were those who made his grave with the wicked ones; yet he was with a rich man in his death, because he had done no violence and there was no fraud in his mouth."[8, 9] Though there were to be men who planned for the Servant's dead body to be disposed of among the corpses of thieves and murderers in the city dump as He had been executed among them, God was to overrule and secure interment in a rich man's tomb ("with the rich"). The reason for this divine providence was to be the Servant's moral purity.

That the Jewish rulers planned for Jesus' body to be thrown to the dogs or into the potter's field the Gospels do not say, but it can scarcely be doubted. The amazing fulfillment of the prophecy of His burial in the tomb of the rich man, Joseph of Arimathea, is told in Matthew 27:57-60.

The last three verses of Isaiah 53 (10-12) are mainly concerned with matters unrelated to visible historical events. The voluntary offering of the Servant's life as an offering to God for the sins of "many" and His being "numbered with transgressors" are the main predictions of a historical nature. There is also the statement in verse 10 that after His death "he shall prolong his days"—a reference to Jesus' resurrection and strong support for Paul's statement in I Corinthians 15:4, "that he rose again the third day according to the scriptures."

This examination, brief and incomplete as it has been, is sufficient to show the unmistakable hand of omniscience in the Bible, "convincing those who have doubted the truth of the Bible, that a prophecy like this demonstrates that the Book in which it occurs must be from God."[10]

So striking is this prophecy that the most desperate means have been employed by unbelievers to destroy its force.

---

[8]The Hebrew is difficult. Though there are precedents for every portion of this translation in standard versions, this is the only one known to the author where all these elements appear in the same translation.

[9]Author's translation, *The Sufferings and the Glory of the Lord's Righteous Servant* (Moline, Ill.: Christian Service Press, 1948), pp. 16, 98.

[10]Albert Barnes, *Notes Critical, Explanatory, and Practical on the Book of Isaiah* (Grand Rapids: Baker Book House reprint), II, 293.

Unbelief has gone so far as to say that the New Testament writers constructed a literary career for Jesus in deliberate correspondence with the prophecy even though His real career was far different. Jewish writers especially use this approach.[10]

Anyone, however, who knows by reading them sympathetically how truthful those New Testament accounts really are, will reject that charge. Men do not die for loyalty to fictitious characters out of literature, even of their own creation, as the authors of the New Testament did for Jesus. Lew Wallace would not have died in service to Ben Hur or Charles Dickens for Tiny Tim. Neither would the apostles have died as martyrs for Jesus if the career which proved Him to be their Messiah had in any sense been their own fictitious creation. Furthermore, the reader should know that New Testament criticism, even in the hands of unbelievers, has come back to a very high view of the historical accuracy of the Gospels.

MICAH 5:2: "But thou, Bethlehem Ephratah, though thou be little among the thousands of Judah, yet out of thee shall he come forth unto me that is to be ruler in Israel; whose goings forth have been from of old, from everlasting."

It was extremely unlikely that a woman living in northern Palestine (Nazareth) would give birth to a child in Bethlehem, several days' traveling time away to the south. Yet according to this seven-centuries-old prophecy, that was where Mary's child should be born. It took an imperial decree from Rome that every citizen in the empire should be properly enrolled in his ancestral locality to bring it about, but so it was (Luke 2:1-6). Micah 5:2, which relates that Messiah was to be an eternal person, also predicts that He would be born in Bethlehem. In accordance with this, as Matthew 2:1-6 informs us, Jewish scholars of the day expected Messiah to be born in Bethlehem.

There is another prophecy which predicts the date of our

Lord's appearing. This accounts for the state of general expectancy of the Saviour at the time of His birth (Dan. 9:24-27). Others predict details of His ministry (Isa. 61:1, 2; cf. Luke 4:14-22). Some prophecies trace recognizable features of the present age (Dan. 2 and 7). The interested reader should consult specialized works on Daniel for further study of this vast field.

About three hundred distinct prophecies of Christ lie in the Old Testament. They were like the pieces of a jigsaw puzzle (except that each presented something distinct which a puzzle piece does not), more or less obscure until Jesus came and put them all in clear relation to one another by His career. It has been calculated that the possibility that these would all be fulfilled in one lifetime by one person is one chance in 84 followed by 131 zeros!

These ten prophecies of Christ have great force as showing the divine origin of Scripture, the Messiahship of Jesus, and the truth of Christianity when viewed together against the whole background of the Old Testament and of the Gospels. Anyone of these alone might be explained away to the satisfaction of antagonistic people, but taken together their force is devastating to unbelief. The weakness of this kind of proof does not lie in the force of the evidence, but in the fact that many modern people are prejudiced against any evidence of the supernatural and are frequently impatient with any effort to introduce such evidence.

### Prophecies Concerning the Nations of Antiquity

Among the prophecies of Scripture are dozens concerning the future of cities, nations, kings, and dynasties. A whole library might be composed in tracing their fulfillment. They begin with predictions in Genesis of such places as Sodom and Gomorrah and Egypt, and end with passages in the Revelation about the whole kingdom of this world. In between, in addition to scattered prophecies in many books, there are twenty consecutive chapters in Isaiah, seventeen chapters in Jeremiah, nine chapters in Ezekiel, and two in Amos. These are "blocks" of prophetic matter concerning the neighboring nations of Israel. In the New Testament there are prophecies of Jesus concerning the cities of Palestine in which He ministered, especially Jerusalem, the destruction of which He graphically and distinctly predicted (Matt. 24; Luke 21; Mark 13).

Perhaps the most impressive case of fulfillment of an Old Testament prophecy of this type is that concerning Tyre in Ezekiel 26. Carefully read the entire chapter. Though the prophecy ends at 28:19, the part in which our interest centers is chapter 26.

In this chapter it is stated that Tyre's malice toward Jerusalem is the occasion for divine wrath upon her (v. 2). There follows a numerous and quite complicated series of specific details about Tyre's destruction.

(1) More than one nation was to have part in fulfilling the coming judgment, for God "will cause many nations to come up against thee" (v. 3).

(2) These nations were to war against the city successively rather than in a united attack, for they would "come up against thee as the sea causeth its waves to come" (v. 3).

(3) There was to be a complete desolation of the city walls, gates, buildings, etc. (vv. 4, 8-14). Many interesting details concerning the methods of ancient siege warfare are introduced here.

(4) The very dust would be scraped away from the site (v. 4).

(5) The destroyers were to make her a bare rock (v. 4).

(6) She "shall be a place for the spreading of nets" (v. 5; cf. v. 14).

(7) "They shall lay thy stones and thy timber and thy dust in the midst of the waters" (v. 12), signifying that somehow

the building and paving materials of old Tyre would wind up in the salty waters of the sea.

(8) The city would never be reconstructed (v. 14).

The picture is further complicated by a quite different prediction of minor chastisement for the neighboring city of Sidon, with continuing existence.

According to the first verse of this prophecy these words were written about the year 586 B.C., very shortly before any of the predictions came to pass. And even if the contention of certain critics were true that Ezekiel's words were spoken, or enlarged by interpolation, after Nebuchadnezzar's siege came to a partially successful conclusion in the following years, some of the most striking details waited more than two centuries for fulfillment.

Here is what happened. In Nebuchadnezzar's time the chief part of Tyre was on the mainland. Offshore half a mile lay a rocky fortified island. As the long (thirteen years) siege by Nebuchadnezzar's armies neared an end, the inhabitants used their superb fleet to remove their possessions to the island city. The Babylonian army utterly wrecked the abandoned city but without gaining plunder, as Ezekiel ironically reports (29:17-20). The stones, timbers, and paving blocks remained in ruined array on the shore for another two and a half centuries. The old city, as Ezekiel had said, was indeed wrecked, but the commercial center offshore continued on, and some pundit of the day might have remarked that it looked as if Nebuchadnezzar did not read all the prophecy! In the ordinary course of events the ruins would become a wind-swept sandy mound or "tell." Who would bother to dump the stuff into the sea and fulfill the rest of the prophecy?

The man was the indomitable Macedonian conqueror, Alexander the Great. In 334 B.C. he led his tough little army across the Hellespont, and, moving across Asia Minor and defeating there in a few months two massive Persian armies, he appeared in the neighborhood of Tyre in 332 B.C. Although the Tyrians were willing to pay him rich tribute, they refused to admit Alexander to their island city. So he and his army set out to conquer it and destroy it.

This is how they did it. They decided to construct a causeway across the channel of deep water separating the old ruined city from the new and to attack it directly. In doing so Alexander unwittingly fulfilled some more of Ezekiel's prophecy, for his army used the materials of the ruins lying on the shore for their jetty. The Tyrians, however, with the use of their fleet, attacked the workmen, drove them off, and destroyed the new work. Alexander then with greater wisdom and mounting fury gathered a fleet from nearby ports and with it protected his workmen while the causeway was under construction. The remainder of the ruins on shore was carted off into the water, the very dust being cast into the works. The island fortress city was then breached, the remaining inhabitants who had not escaped to the far western colony at Carthage either slain or sold as slaves, and Tyre came to an end—thus fulfilling Ezekiel's prophecy.

Sidon, to the contrary, though quite as vulnerable to invaders, and although attacked and conquered many times, subsequently was not obliterated, and continues to the present day.

Although there is now a town of Tyre in the vicinity of the ancient city, it has no connection with the old city which is long since gone. Fishermen have used the spot for generations for the spreading of their nets, just as Ezekiel said. A little digging in the stretch that juts out into the sea at the spot will discover the very stones that the Macedonian armies cast into the sea.

Another remarkable portion of this sort is Zechariah 9:1-8. It is so specific and detailed in its predictions all fulfilled— that it alone is sufficient to demonstrate the possibility of predictive prophecy. In these verses the success of Alexander the Great's invasion of Syria and Palestine in the seventh decade of the fourth century B.C. is set forth in detail. Of course, it is in the poetic style of prophecy rather than the prose of history, but none the less specific. In fact, Zechariah 9-14 is in large part predictions regarding Alexander's campaign along the eastern Mediterranean littoral from Phoenicia to Egypt and of the subsequent fortunes of the Jews until the time of Jesus. The reading of these six chapters with the help of a good evangelical commentary (we recommend Henderson) is a most reassuring experience.

Zechariah 9:1-8 tells how Alexander would absorb Syria with its cities of Hamath and Damascus. Then Tyre would be obliterated and her commerce destroyed, to the amazement of her neighbors. Sidon, though mentioned with Tyre, is not to share in this desolation. Further down the coastal line of march in Philistine territory the cities Gaza, Ekron, Ashkelon, and Ashdod would be frightened, then captured. Only Gath, lying farther inland and out of the line of march, is omitted among the five great Philistine cities. A foreigner was to be king of Ashdod. Ultimately the Philistines were to become Jewish proselytes as had the ancient Jebusites in David's time. The Jews were to be spared the anger of Alexander.

Josephus' account of the march of Alexander shows how minutely that portion was fulfilled. The story of the Maccabees and how they compelled the inhabitants of their southern neighboring countries to accept circumcision or die, fills out the story.

## THE CASE OF THE JEWISH PEOPLE

We have saved till last the most remarkable case of fulfillment of prophecy concerning a nation of antiquity—the case of the Jewish people. According to a well-known story, Frederick the Great of Prussia, a famous doubter, once asked his court chaplain, "Give me in one word a proof of the truth of the Bible." The answer was simply, "The Jews."

God chose them not because they were big, good, or famous (Deut. 7:7, 8), but simply on account of His sovereign love. Moses predicted that from time to time they would be scattered from their land on account of unbelief and disobedience (Deut. 28:36, 63 ff.). In dispersion they would be "an astonishment, a proverb, and a byword, among all nations whither the LORD shall lead them" (Deut. 28:37). Yet they were not to be scattered "to destroy them utterly" (see Lev. 26, esp. verses 43-46). They would later return. The northern tribes were so evicted about 722 B.C. (II Kings 17), and the mass of them have remained in dispersion to the present day. In a series of deportations from 605 to 586 B.C. the Babylonians took away the Jewish inhabitants of southern Palestine. Yet according to Moses' general prediction they were to return, and according to the prophecies of Jeremiah this was to take place in about seventy years (Jer. 25:11; cf. Dan. 9:1, 2). And they did return, as reported in Ezra, Nehemiah and several of the minor prophets.

They were still in Palestine when Jesus was born. Yet He predicted that their holy Jerusalem was soon to be destroyed (Matt. 24:1, 2) and that they would again be scattered. These things all took place within about a century. Yet Jesus also said that the nation of Israel would endure to the very end of this age (Matt. 24:34); the apostles expected their kingdom to return (Acts 1:6); Paul predicts their future conversion and restoration to divine favor (Rom. 11, esp. verse 26). The last book of the Bible states that the Jews as a people will yet behold Jesus their Messiah and mourn for Him (Rev. 1:7), and a host of Old Testament predictions indicate that they shall again possess their land (see esp. Jer. 31).

It is just possible that we are seeing in the well-known recent events in Jewry and in Palestine the fulfillment, in part, of these prophecies. "Behold, he that keepeth Israel shall neither slumber nor sleep" (Ps. 121:4). "Thus saith the Lord, which giveth the sun for a light by day, and the ordinances of the moon and of the stars for a light by night, which divideth the sea when the waves thereof roar; The Lord of hosts is his name: if those ordinances depart from before me, saith the Lord, then the seed of Israel also shall cease from being a nation before me for ever" (Jer. 31:35, 36). So the history of Israel through the centuries is a story of remarkable prophecy and its remarkable fulfillment.

These facts and many others testify that in our Bible we have the powerful Word of the omniscient God who declares "the end from the beginning, and from ancient times the things that are not yet done, saying, My counsel shall stand, and I will do all my pleasure . . . yea, I have spoken it. I will also bring it to pass; I have purposed it, I will also do it" (Isa. 46:10, 11).

Even by using the most extreme tactics it is impossible to date a large number of the Old Testament prophecies so late that they may be considered mere historical accounts rather than predictions. And once we conclude that many of these prophecies are truly prophetic, the whole narrative of human history becomes a vast account of their fulfillment and a vast demonstration of the power and foreknowledge of God and of the truth of His Word.

*Chapter 6*

# HOW RELIABLE IS THE OLD TESTAMENT TEXT?

*by*

R. LAIRD HARRIS

## Chapter 6

# HOW RELIABLE IS THE
# OLD TESTAMENT
# TEXT?

IF YOU GO to Washington, D.C., you can see in the Archives building the original Declaration of Independence. It is carefully preserved under glass, away from strong light, so that it will last a long time. You can still see the signatures of John Hancock and the other signers. Many people see this exhibit every day. But really it is of no special value except as a curiosity, for we have plenty of very accurate copies of the Declaration.

In the case of the Old Testament, we no longer have the original documents written by Moses, Isaiah, Ezra and the others. They lived a long time ago and the ravages of time plus wars, persecutions, and neglect have destroyed the originals. But we have copies. The question before us in this chapter is, how good are our copies? How close are our copies to that which was written by David and others under the inspiration of the Holy Spirit?

This is what we call textual criticism. It studies the reliability of the text. It is to be sharply distinguished from destructive higher criticism, which argues, usually on subjective grounds, that certain passages in the books were inserted by a later author, that the books were not written by the author who claimed to write them, and that the books are generally untrustworthy. Higher criticism has brought a wave of disbelief in the Bible. Textual criticism is quite different. It is the study of the copying of ancient manuscripts. As such it is a little technical and requires us to put ourselves in the shoes (or sandals) of an ancient scribe to see how he worked.

Textual criticism of the New Testament has been thoroughly studied and great and orthodox men have been engaged in it for years. But textual critical study of the Old Testament has not been so widely taken up, especially by orthodox men. In a short treatment, we cannot really study it; we can only learn something of its principles and its results.

### Principles and Results

To put ourselves in the place of an ancient scribe we would have to lock up our typewriters, close all printed books, drop our fountain pens and burn all our modern paper. Then we would have to learn Hebrew. Perhaps this is why not many people study textual criticism of the Old Testament! But you can't understand ancient Hebrew copying until you understand Hebrew—and ancient Hebrew at that. So we shall have to learn something, at least, about Hebrew.

Hebrew, or the Canaanite language, was spoken at a very early period in Canaan. Probably Abraham did not know it until he move into Palestine. We do not have any Hebrew writing of Abraham's day. The Babylonian writing of that day was wedge-shaped marks on clay tablets to indicate syllables. The Egyptian writing used pictures for words. But shortly after Abraham's day some Canaanites made an important invention. They invented the alphabet, which greatly simplified the process of learning to write. The sign for a letter was a rough sketch of an object which began with that letter. Thus "b" was pictured by a floor plan of a house because in Canaanite "house" began with "b." This alphabet was carried by the Phoenicians to Greece and is the mother of nearly all our alphabets today.

There was one problem. No Canaanite words began with vowels, so no letters of this kind were invented. For two thousand years Hebrew was written without a real system of vowels. It would be difficult for us to write English without vowels. The letters "bd" could mean "bad," "bed," "bid," "bud," "bade," "bide." This is not so in Hebrew, since it is not so ambiguous without vowels as English is. The consonants "ktb" in Hebrew mean "write." They could mean "to write" or "he wrote" or "writing" or "something written," but Hebrew does not have the ambiguity of English where "bk" could mean "book" or "bike." So Hebrew did not need the vowels as much as we would think. A good Hebrew student can read Hebrew without the vowels with very little uncertainty.

Yet vowels assist in distinguishing different forms of verbs and nouns. It is helpful to be able to distinguish "qtl"—"he is killing" — from "qtl"—"he is killed"! So eventually certain consonants, which in some places became silent, like "y" and "w" and "h," were used to indicate the more important vowels. These we call "vowel letters." Finally, but only in the Middle Ages, did the Hebrew scribes invent a system of dots and dashes to indicate the vowels scientifically. These are placed above and below the letters and are called "vowel points" or "pointing."

It can be seen that Hebrew writing passed through three stages. In Moses' day, only the consonants were written. By the end of the Old Testament period in Ezra's day, the vowel letters could be used more or less freely to indicate the important vowels. In post-Christian days the sacred text had vowel points added to it by Jewish scribes, and these are used in the Hebrew Bibles today.

It seems obvious that in textual criticism, since we are interested in the original copies, we can largely discount the vowel points. They were not written by the prophets and are not inspired. It is true that the vowel pointing has been carefully done and we should not entirely disregard it, but we are not bound by it. But what about the consonantal text? How close is it to the original? How carefully has the copying been done?

To answer this question we must go to the museums where old manuscripts are kept. But there has been one disadvantage. Until recently we had no very old copies of the Hebrew Old Testament even in museums. It appears that the Jews of the Middle Ages reverently destroyed their worn-out copies of the Scriptures. Fortunately they prepared new copies with utmost care. If in copying a scroll they made too many mistakes they branded the copy unfit for official use. They counted the words and the verses and figured the middle verse of a book so as to prevent careless dropping of anything. From all this, it seems clear that although there are no copies older than about A.D. 900, still the text had been preserved very faithfully since at least A.D. 100 or 200. Indeed, comparison with some translations made into Greek and Latin around A.D. 200 to 400 proves that the Hebrew text was copied very carefully all that time.

All of our present copies of the Hebrew text coming from A.D. 900 and later are in remarkably close agreement. The scribes did a splendid job of proofreading. The fact is that comparison of one manuscript with another is not very valuable for they are all almost identical. The main differences concern the vowel letters and other small details of spelling. This unified text, the product of the Jewish scribes known as "Massoretes," is called the "Massoretic Text," or M.T. for short.

However, there naturally was uncertainty about the state of the text in pre-Massoretic times. Before A.D. 200 the Jews apostatized into a cold, formalistic Pharisaism. They were driven out of Palestine in the Roman invasion of A.D. 70. Before that there were the civil wars of the first century B.C. and the Maccabean wars of independence after 168 B.C. How careful were copyists during these silent centuries? Did they reverence the Scriptures as much then, and did they copy them extensively and preserve them carefully?

## Contribution of the Dead Sea Scrolls

In the providence of God, we now have an answer to these questions. In the hot, dry valley of the Dead Sea, a little south of ancient Jericho, the famous Dead Sea Scrolls were discovered in 1947 and later. It seems that in the period from about 150 B.C. to A.D. 70 a colony of Jews lived at Qumran and operated it very much like a monastery. They shared all their possessions in common, worked the fields nearby, and spent their time copying and studying the Scriptures. When it became clear that the Romans were going to invade, they put their valuable leather scrolls in jars and hid them in caves in the side of the cliffs that rise west of the Dead Sea toward the mountains of Jerusalem. Several of the caves have now been discovered, first by accident and then by exploration. The result is that for the first time we have Hebrew manuscripts from pre-Christian times with which to compare our Hebrew Massoretic Text.

The material of the Dead Sea caves is extensive and has been much discussed.[1] We are not here concerned with the non-Biblical items, but only with the copies of the Old Testament books. There are fragments of almost every book in the Old Testament. Some books are found in several fragmentary copies and large portions of some books are preserved. The book of Isaiah is preserved in one complete copy (copy a) and another tattered copy which has much of Isaiah 38-66 (copy b). The books of Samuel have been largely preserved in a tattered copy which has not yet been fully studied and published. Two chapters of Habakkuk have been preserved complete, embedded in a commentary. Other portions, though smaller, are very significant for study. They

[1]For a good introductory discussion, see Charles F. Pfeiffer, *The Dead Sea Scrolls* (Grand Rapids: Baker Book House, 1957).

give firsthand evidence as to the accuracy of ancient copying.

For example, we may study the copy b of Isaiah. The text is extremely close to our M.T. A comparison of Isaiah 53 shows that only seventeen letters differ from M.T. Ten of these are mere differences of spelling, like our "honor" or "honour," and make no change at all in meaning. Four more are very minor differences, such as the presence of the conjunction which is often a matter of style. The other three letters are the Hebrew word for "light" which is added after "they shall see" in verse 11. Out of 166 words in this chapter only this one word is really in question and it does not at all change the sense of the passage.

This is typical of the whole manuscript. Even the use of vowel letters and the preservation of archaic grammatical forms are exceedingly close to the M.T. It is true that the manuscript is not perfect. There are two or three places where the copyist skipped a few words because his eye jumped from one word to one just like it in the line below. This is a frequent error of copying as any typist realizes. Slips like this show that it is wise always to check one copy against another. But the manuscript dating from the first century B.C. is so much like the M.T. that we must marvel at the accuracy of the scribes who worked in the succeeding centuries.

The other Isaiah scroll (copy a) is complete. Although it is a bit older (about 125 B.C.) than copy b, it seems to represent a later stage of the text. It shows an extensive use of the vowel letters which seem to reflect the pronunciation current in its time, whereas copy b preserves the older, simple spelling. Comparing Isaiah 53 again, we find that aside from spelling differences, the two scrolls differ only in seven places. Six of these are the presence or absence of the conjunction "and," which in Hebrew is the single prefixed letter "w." In the seventh case the manuscript is blurred, and corrected. It is not clear whether the preposition "with" is written—a synonym of the preposition "with" used in copy b—or whether an extraneous word is inserted. In any case the two manuscripts are very very close together and very close to the M.T. Actually, copy a is usually said to be a poor copy of the type of text appearing in the M.T. Like copy b it has a few mistakes of accidental omission of words. It seems clear that the M.T. has very carefully preserved a type of text that was current in the second century B.C. Other fragments, e.g., of Leviticus, lead us to say that the whole Old Testament at that early time existed in copies using the Massoretic type of text.

But we have other ancient witnesses. For many years we have had the Greek translation of the Old Testament called the Septuagint (abbreviated LXX because it was supposed to have been done by seventy Jewish scholars). The date of the LXX is in dispute. Legend says it was translated or at least the Pentateuch was done by 250 B.C. It is referred to in the apocryphal book Ecclesiasticus, written by 130 B.C., as widely known in that time. A fair date seems to be about 200 B.C. Though our copies of the Septuagint come from post-Christian times we can use it to find out the Hebrew text from which it was translated about 200 B.C. Only we must use it with caution.

Up to now we were never sure of the reason for variation when the LXX differed from the M.T. Was it that the M.T. had changed since 200 B.C.? Or had the Septuagint translators done a poor job? Or had the Septuagint changed since 200 B.C.? Now the Dead Sea Scrolls help answer the problem. First, as we have seen, the M.T. has not changed to speak of since 200 B.C. But furthermore, other scrolls have been found which look very much like the Hebrew from which the LXX was translated. Especially the Samuel scroll is said to resemble closely the reading of the LXX. Some of the other fragments seem to be the same type of text. Apparently the LXX was translated rather literally and apparently our manuscripts are pretty good copies of the original translation. The evidence of the scrolls shows that already in 200 B.C. the original Hebrew Old Testament had been copied and recopied to such an extent that different main types of text had developed. There was the M.T. type and the LXX type, and there is some evidence for a third type close to that preserved by the Samaritans, who to this day keep some old scrolls of the Pentateuch in their colony of Nablus in Palestine.

We therefore can trace out these types of text in circulation in 200 B.C. This situation is much like that of the New Testament field where we can identify three or four families of text existent around A.D. 300. As manuscripts were copied and recopied, mistakes of a few early parent copies tended to get preserved in the later ages and families of manuscripts, each with its own characteristic readings, began to form. Today, with the help of the Massoretic Text, the Septuagint, and the Samaritan Pentateuch, we can reconstruct the three main families of text that were once current in 200 B.C.

### Hebrew or Greek?

We are therefore somewhat in the position of a scholar of 200 B.C. In our endeavor to arrive at the original reading of the Old Testament we have three families of text to choose from. How shall we do it? Shall we compare and decide that the M.T. is the best? Probably most scholars would say that the M.T. on the whole is best, but there are some places where simple comparison shows that the LXX is better. Significantly the New Testament quotations often, indeed usually, follow the LXX. So actually a good textual critic will now compare all three types of text and where they differ will try to come to a decision as to which reading is more likely to be correct. This study calls for care and good judgment and must proceed upon certain definite principles, but solid results can often be obtained and it is rewarding. After all, our witness is now only a couple of centuries later than the days of Ezra the scribe, who according to Jewish tradition edited the Scriptures and brought them out in a form with which we should surely be well satisfied.

However, as we have pointed out elsewhere,[2] the purpose of textual criticism is not only to arrive, if possible, at the original reading. Sometimes it is not possible to be absolutely sure whether a particular word or phrase should be added or deleted. The additional purpose of textual criticism is to evaluate our present texts to see how close to the original they are. Is the Septuagint so closely parallel to the Massoretic Text that it matters little which one we choose?

It may be well to be specific. If we carry on our comparison of Isaiah 53, we find that the differences of the LXX with the Dead Sea Scroll of Isaiah, copy b, concern about twenty words. Of these, seven are the conjunction, which often is, as we have seen, a stylistic variation. As to the other variations, some idea of the differences should be given.

The Greek begins the chapter with the words "O Lord." It translates the first word of verse 1, "we brought a report," which probably is a free rendering of the Hebrew text. It omits "God" in verse 4, in the phrase, "smitten of God, and afflicted." It omits "despised" in verse 3. In verse 8 it renders "from prison" as "in humiliation," which again is probably a free translation. Also in verse 11, two words are taken somewhat differently, though not changing the sense. Aside from these, there are a few differences in treating the pronoun endings of the Hebrew words.

We cannot go into detail in this discussion and it is difficult to appreciate the whole picture without reference to the Hebrew and Greek, but it should be clear that the Septuagint text is in good general agreement with the Massoretic Text.

[2]R. Laird Harris, *Inspiration and Canonicity of the Bible* (Grand Rapids: Zondervan Publishing House, 1957), pp. 90-95.

No doctrinal differences are involved here. It is not a slavishly literal translation, but yet seems to agree very closely with the Massoretic Text. It is true that occasionally in other places the Septuagint departs further from the Massoretic Text than here. But still the differences are almost always the small matters of freedom in translation, stylistic variations, minor copying errors, and struggling with difficult Hebrew, which interest the scholars yet make no significant difference in the use and meaning of the passage. The fact is that if we discarded our Hebrew Bibles, the Septuagint, though sounding strange in places, would be a very satisfactory copy of the Old Testament. Indeed, for the first three centuries of the Christian church when most Christians spoke Greek fluently, the Septuagint was used almost exclusively.

The new information of the Dead Sea Scrolls shows that the Septuagint reflects a type of Hebrew text slightly different from our Massoretic Text. By comparing the two we can now correct and improve our Massoretic Text in spots, for after all, two witnesses are better than one. Yet the fact remains that whether in any particular verse we choose the LXX reading or the M.T., we still will not go far wrong, for they are not far apart. They are the same Bible, the product of careful scribal copying in those years back of 200 B.C., reaching on to Ezra's time and probably even before. Some scholars are now suggesting that perhaps our M.T. is a copy of the manuscripts Ezra used, which doubtless were very carefully prepared, whereas the LXX may represent a copy of some older private manuscript in existence before the Babylonian captivity. This is not impossible, though it can hardly be proved.

The new emphasis on the LXX is of special interest because in most instances the New Testament quotes the Old Testament in the LXX form. In a few cases this introduces a discrepancy where the wording of the LXX is not like that of the

M.T. Dead Sea material has supported the LXX in several of these cases and thus cleared up old problems of detail. For instance, in Hebrews 1:6 there is a quotation from Deuteronomy 32:43 which was found only in the LXX. New Dead Sea fragments show that old Hebrew copies also had this clause, and thus the LXX here preserves the correct text which is followed in the New Testament.

There are only two major places where the LXX departs from the M.T. One is that our later copies of the LXX include the apocryphal books. This we discuss under the question of canon.[3] The fact is that we have no evidence to show that the earlier Jewish copyists of the LXX included these apocryphal books in their sacred collection. They probably did not. At least the Jews of Palestine clearly did not.

The second variation comes in the book of Jeremiah, which lacks almost sixty verses in the LXX. At first this seems to be quite a defect, but closer scrutiny shows that many of these are duplicate verses which occur again elsewhere in Jeremiah or other Old Testament books, and therefore the LXX of Jeremiah actually has nearly all that the Hebrew has. This is of special interest, because again Dead Sea fragments have been discovered supporting the LXX text of Jeremiah and showing some of these omissions. This raises the possibility that the LXX form of Jeremiah is the original one, and these duplicate verses were inserted by some scribe for special purposes. At least there is no essential difference between the LXX and M.T. even in Jeremiah except that a few chapters are in a different order.

We are now ready to come to some conclusions about the text of the Old Testament. Fortunately we have new facts on which to base our conclusions—facts not available until recent years.

We can now be sure that copyists worked with great care and accuracy on the Old Testament even back to 225 B.C.

[3]See Chapter 4, page 8.

At that time there were two or three types of text available for copying. These types differed among themselves so little, however, that we can infer that still earlier copyists had also faithfully and carefully transmitted the Old Testament text. Indeed it would be rash skepticism that would now deny we have our Old Testament in a form very close to that used by Ezra when he taught the law to those who had returned from Babylonian captivity.

## High Quality of Biblical Manuscripts

We have no Old Testament manuscripts from the time before Ezra, but three additional lines of evidence confirm our conclusion that our copies are actually good copies of the books that left the hands of the ancient prophets.

First we have the evidence from archaeology. This is extensive and has been given fully in other books,[4] but we shall give an illustration. Not only does archaeology confirm Old Testament history in general, it also confirms many small details of the Biblical record. One interesting case is Bible names. Names are not easy to remember or to copy. Foreign names especially are easily corrupted. The Old Testament includes many names of Israel's kings and of foreign kings from the Pharaohs of Egypt to the Persian rulers. How are these preserved? The answer is, wonderfully well. Great kings like Shishak, obscure men like Sanballat, Hebrew names like Omri, Assyrian names like Sargon, all are well preserved and practically letter perfect. Names of ancient lands and forgotten people are preserved. The Hebrew for "Horite" is a precise rendering of the ethnical name "Hurrian" which was used by a people long forgotten. The name "Shinar" in Hebrew is closer to the old name of the land of the Sumerians than is our current designation "Sumer." In

[4]*Cf.* Joseph P. Free, *Archaeology and Bible History* (Wheaton, Ill.: Scripture Press, 1956), and Robert Dick Wilson, *A Scientific Investigation of the Old Testament.* Revised edition by E. J. Young (Chicago: Moody Press, 1959), especially pp. 66-76.

Jeremiah 39:3 the Hebrew text gives what appears to be six names of Nebuchadnezzar's officers. These men were unknown till recently. Archaeology now shows that they were three officers, but each had his title given: Nergalsharezer of Samgar-nebo; Nebo-Sarsechim, the Rab-saris; and Nergal-Sharezer, the Rab-mag. But every letter of the Hebrew has been transmitted correctly.

A second evidence of faithful copying is found in the transmission of parallel texts. Perhaps many do not realize how many duplicate passages there are in the Old Testament. Several psalms occur twice in the book or are in the historical books as well as among the Psalms. Much of Isaiah 32-39 is also found in II Kings and large parts of Chronicles are found in Samuel and Kings and elsewhere. A study of these passages is interesting. It can be done in the English Bible itself. Compare, for instance, Isaiah 2:2-4 with Micah 4:1-3. The correspondence is almost exact. The last chapter of Jeremiah compared with II Kings 25 shows that Jeremiah has added (or Kings has dropped) a number of explanatory words here and there, but the agreement is close. Some of the differences that exist may well have been due to the freedom of the original authors in their quoting one another's work. But if the differences are totally due to copyists, still we would have to say that the copyists have been accurate and careful in their work.

One last line of evidence is general. We can compare the Hebrew scribes with the Babylonian ones. Babylonian scribes also copied old documents. We have an original copy of King Hammurabi's great law code given about 1700 B.C. and we have copies of it on clay tablets dating from a thousand years later. The correspondence is very close. It is dangerous to generalize too easily, but the conclusion seems to be that the scribes of antiquity were as a rule careful in their work—that's what they were paid for. A former generation of destructive critics talked much about mistakes of "sleepy scribes." Mistakes there were, of course, but presumably scribes that were habitually sleepy got fired! The scribes were paid to be careful copyists and were trained in their work. Egyptian sources emphasize that it was a respected profession. Presumably Jewish scribes who reverenced their law were the more careful to do a good job.

We may conclude our rather technical study of the Old Testament text by saying that new evidence as well as older study gives us adequate grounds for saying that the sacred text of the Hebrew Old Testament is completely reliable. With modern evidence, it can be improved slightly in spots and this even helps to clear up some problems in a few New Testament quotations. But by and large, we are fully justified in saying concerning the Old Testament what Westcott and Hort said concerning the New: except for trivialities, not one part in a thousand is in serious doubt and we have no objective evidence to make us think that doctrinal differences or substantial matters are involved in the whole process of Old Testament copying.

*Chapter* 7

# IS THE HISTORY OF THE OLD TESTAMENT ACCURATE?

*by*

MEREDITH G. KLINE

*Chapter 7*

# IS THE HISTORY OF THE OLD TESTAMENT ACCURATE?

WHAT ONE THINKS about the accuracy of Old Testament history will be influenced by what he thinks about some larger questions. Old Testament history is one miracle after another. To the aged and barren, children are born. Angels appear and walk the rugged terrain of Palestine. Coming events are foretold. The finger of God inscribes divine law on tables of stone. A miraculous glory-cloud leads Israel through the wilderness. Without this supernatural strand, Old Testament history would not be Old Testament history at all.

Consequently, even if enough evidence were available from archaeology and related sciences to vouch for all the ordinary data (chronological, political, etc.), the history in the Old Testament would still appear radically distorted to those who regard the idea of divine intervention in human affairs as nonsense. Similarly, the *view* of history embedded in the Old Testament is not the sort of thing archaeology is able to verify. The Old Testament's interpretation of the movement of history will call forth agreement or disagreement according to the reader's total life and world view. For example, when the Old Testament interprets the events of the Exodus and Conquest in terms of God's showing favor to Israel at the expense of other people, such as the Egyptians and Canaanites, some readers might judge that interpretation to be a distasteful display of Israelite arrogance. It is, therefore, futile to tackle the defense of the various external details without first facing up to the deeper issues of Christian supernaturalism—of God, His creation and redemptive revelation—and of truth, what it is and how it can be known.

These fundamental issues cannot be dealt with, however, within the limits of this chapter. It must suffice to state here that apart from the God of the infallible Word, truth would be lost in meaningless darkness through which there would never resound the creative word, "Let there be light," separating the light from the darkness and assigning to each its definition as "Day" or "Night." And apart from the infallible, absolutely authoritative Word of God, man's quest for truth would be a hopeless writhing to escape the coils of subjectivism and historical relativism. The necessary presupposition for the writing of this book or for predication of any kind is the God of the infallible Word.

When we affirm the perfect historical accuracy of the Old Testament, we are not claiming that our favorite English version of it or even our best critical Hebrew text is infallible. Our claim is only that the original manuscripts were without error. But while it is useful to realize that we do not possess the original infallible text down to the last detail, it is unwarranted to conclude that it is unimportant whether there ever were a completely accurate text, as though a generally trustworthy Bible would suffice.

The point has been illustrated this way: Suppose we try to drive over a river when its flooding waters have risen above the level of the bridge. To drive across the bridge we must drive through a few inches of water. Not ideal conditions; we can manage, however. But if the bridge were non-existent, crossing the river would be utterly impossible. "What the idea of general trustworthiness without infallible inspiration does in effect is to say that it really makes no difference whether there is a solid bottom under us, inasmuch as we have to drive through water in any case. But we have seen that man needs absolutely authoritative interpretation."[1]

Furthermore, the available evidence—not least that of the Dead Sea Scrolls—confirms the verdict of the Westminster Assemby theologians, who confessed that the inspired Scriptures were by God's "singular care and providence kept pure in all ages."[2] The most prominent Biblical archaeologist of our day writes: "We may rest assured that the consonantal text of the Hebrew Bible, though not infallible, has been preserved with an accuracy perhaps unparalleled in any other Near-Eastern literature."[3] You might say that so far as the historical accuracy of the Old Testament is concerned, that bridge across the river has only a few small puddles on it. Unfortunately, rationalistic scholars, like little boys, delight in getting the biggest and muddiest splash possible out of small puddles.

To take our stand humbly with those whose eyes God has opened to recognize the perfect truthfulness of the Word He has spoken, does not mean that we are committed to all the woodenly literalistic interpretation that has been imposed on the Old Testament. But great caution is necessary at this point lest warning against one error, a far worse error be encouraged. The "worse error" we refer to is found in the dominant theological movement of our day, Barthianism, which denies the real, literal historicity of the key events recorded in Scripture.

Take in particular their treatment of the history in Gene-

[1]Cornelius Van Til, *An Introduction to Systematic Theology* (unpublished class syllabus), 1951, p. 148. For all the broader apologetic issues mentioned above, see C. Van Til, *The Defense of the Faith* (Philadelphia: Presbyterian and Reformed Publishing Co., 1955).

[2]The Westminster Confession of Faith, chap. 1, sec. 8.

[3]W. F. Albright in *The Old Testament and Modern Study*, ed. H .H. Rowley (New York: Oxford University Press, 1951), p. 25, citing W. F. Albright.

sis. It is assumed with negative higher criticism in general that Genesis as we know it is the product of late Israelite editors who pieced together various older sources. But the distinctive feature of the new approach is that these editors are supposed to have infused a new meaning into the ancient stories. As incorporated into Genesis, the purpose of such stories, it is said, is not to portray specific past events of history on this earth, such as the Fall of a real Adam and Eve in an actual garden in Eden, but only to point to some suprahistorical aspect of the experience of Everyman. The practical consequence is that the reins of Barthian interpretation are let loose and it runs amuck over the sacred records, dissolving Biblical history in the acid of theological allegorization—allegorization as unwarranted and undisciplined as its older, less sophisticated cousins.[4]

## Archaeology's Role in Demonstrating Bible Accuracy

What now of archaeology's contribution to our subject? How has it influenced the climate of scholarly opinion concerning the accuracy of Old Testament history? Evangelicals usually and most effectively answer this question by pointing out how archaeological discoveries have compelled even negative critics to repudiate the radical theories of the nineteenth century leader of higher criticism, Julius Wellhausen. His attack on the reliability of the Old Testament was not confined to details here and there, but was directed against the over-all structure of its history of Israel. That is seen plainly in his suggested reconstruction along evolutionary lines of the development of the Old Testament literature itself. In place of the Biblical sequence of Mosaic Law and

[4]The best critical analysis of Barthianism is C. Van Til, *Christianity and Barthianism* (Philadelphia: Presbyterian and Reformed Publishing Co., 1962). On the vital issue of the genuine historicity of redemptive history see J. G. Machen, *Christianity and Liberalism* (Grand Rapids: Wm. B. Eerdmans Publishing Co., 1923), and E. J. Young, *The Study of Old Testament Theology Today* (London: James Clarke and Co., 1958), pp. 13 ff.

Prophets, Wellhausen substituted the new order of Prophets followed by non-Mosaic Law. That of course involved the most drastic rejection of the Bible's picture of the Mosaic age and obviously also of the still earlier patriarchal age. The Bible's description of those times was regarded as totally inaccurate, a product of first millennium B.C. authors, who imaginatively projected the conditions of their own day back into the dim, prehistoric second millennium B.C.

The story of twentieth century Biblical archaeology is the story of the silencing of the clamorous voice of the modern western Wellhausen by the voiceless witnesses emerging from ancient eastern mounds. The plot of the story would be clearer were it not for the reluctance of critical scholars to part with their traditional teachings. But all are now obliged to admit that far from the Biblical narratives of patriarchal and Mosaic days being alien to the second millennium B.C. where the Biblical chronology locates them, they would be completely out of place in the first millennium B.C. The Biblical sequence of Law and Prophets has been vindicated.[5]

The pull of archaeology in the opposite polar direction from Wellhausen criticism is evident in the tensions that exist in current critical views of the Pentateuch. It is allowed by critical scholars that the supposed Pentateuchal documents are based on very old sources, and it is admitted that these preserved accurately the ancient historical background (a confession archaeology demands). But it is still maintained that the final editing of the documents is the work of late editors of approximately the same dates as Wellhausen assigned to them (a concession to the pontifical utterances of pre-archaeological higher criticism). Again, there is stress on the astonishing accuracy of oral tradition, to

[5]For a comprehensive and masterly critique of the higher criticism of the Pentateuch see O. T. Allis, *The Five Books of Moses* (Philadelphia: Presbyterian and Reformed Publishing Co., second edition, 1949).

which criticism traces the earliest origins of the Biblical narratives. But over against this a continuing radical wing is still so negative that all it acknowledges to be known for certain about so recent a figure as Moses is that he died—which, as someone has remarked, would seem to be a reasonable assumption.

Illustrations may now be given of particular archaeological evidence which increases our appreciation of the historical accuracy of the Old Testament. We will focus upon the history of the second millennium B.C. because that has been the object of the most severe criticism (except for the still earlier history recorded in Gen. 1-11).[6] Moreover, a general evaluation has already been given concerning the relevance of archaeology for that period and it would be well to cite some substantiating facts. Even with the limits reduced to the second millennium, only a few highlights can be mentioned here.

## Archaeological Support for Biblical Dates

Since man is a creature of time, the student of his history is plagued with dates—dates to be memorized, dates to be discovered too. Determining the dates of Moses and the patriarchs would seem fairly simple, for there is in the Old Testament an abundance of precise chronological data covering the period from Abraham to Solomon (for whose date

[6]The author of this chapter has dealt in published articles with two of the major problems in the early part of Genesis. See the *Westminster Theological Journal*, May 1958 (XX, 2, pp. 146-157) and May 1962 (XXIV, 2, pp. 187-204) for discussions of the chronology of creation and the alleged myth of the sons of God in Genesis 6:1-4. Limitations of space allow for only a comment or two here. As for Genesis 1, the traditional types of exegesis are guilty of laying a man-made stumbling block in the path of modern students, for it is exegetically demonstrable that the *chronological data* of Genesis 1:1—2:3 are to be interpreted figuratively rather than as a literal description of either the duration or sequence of the creation history. Neither should the question of the antiquity of man disturb anyone's confidence in the Scriptures, for the genealogies of Genesis 5 and 11 are manifestly not intended to be complete. The Biblical data provide only a minimum, not maximum possible date for both the Flood and the creation of man.

there is a scholarly agreement within about a decade). That period lasted a little over a millennium, according to the Biblical chronology. But radical scholars would shrink it to half a millennium! Even some more moderate critics have insisted that the Biblical figures are a century or two off. They allow Abraham no earlier a date than the nineteenth or twentieth century B.C. whereas the Bible places his birth at Ur in the twenty-second century B.C. and the sojourning of the three patriarchs (Abraham, Isaac, and Jacob) in Canaan in the twenty-first to nineteenth centuries. Likewise, the Bible's fifteenth-century date for Moses and the Exodus is almost universally rejected in favor of a thirteenth century date.

It would be an easy solution to assume that the chronological figures given in the Bible are no more than round numbers never intended to be taken literally. Unfortunately the matter is more complicated than that. For example, if one dates the Exodus in the thirteenth century, he must synchronize the Biblical narrative with the history of the nineteenth dynasty of Egyptian pharaohs. In doing so he finds it necessary to reject fact after fact in the Mosaic account as unhistorical. Moses' life span must at best be cut in half and then there is no room left for the whole long episode of the Exodus-generation of Israelites wandering and perishing in the wilderness.

It is all the more significant, then, that archaeological confirmation of the Biblical dates is accumulating. Exploration in the Negeb (the southern part of Canaan which was the major center of patriarchal life) reveals that the residence of the patriarchs there could have occurred only in the twenty-first to the nineteenth centuries B.C. An agricultural population had settlements in the Negeb during that period, but from the eighteenth century onward the area was oc-

cupied by wild Bedouin.[7] Now, if the Biblical chronology
is found to be so precisely accurate for the Middle Bronze
Age (roughly 2000–1500 B.C.), even scholars without the
presuppositions of consistent Christian theism should be
ready to respect the Biblical chronology of the Late Bronze
Age (about 1500–1200 B.C.) and the concluding phases of
the second millennium B.C.

Vindication of the Bible's fifteenth-century date for Israel's journeying under Moses comes from Amman, capital
of modern Jordan. One of the persistent objections to the
Biblical dating was that, allegedly, organized kingdoms with
a settled culture did not exist in the Transjordan area from
the eighteenth to the thirteenth century B.C. and accordingly
the resistance which Israel encountered as Moses led them
through the territory of Edom, Moab, and Ammon could
have been no earlier than the thirteenth century. As a
result, however, of an accidental discovery made by bull-
dozers preparing an airfield at Amman, an excavation was
recently undertaken which indicated there was a settled oc-
cupation in Ammon, at least, from *circa* 1550 onward.[8]

The fact that tribal Semites such as modern Arab nomads
memorize long personal genealogies but keep no track of
birthdays and are poor at reckoning years (a fact sometimes
cited as a reason for mistrusting the Biblical chronological
data), only makes the Bible's demonstrable accuracy the
more remarkable.

The period during which the patriarchs passed their lives
in Canaan was no pre-historic era unacquainted with the ac-
complishments of a mature settled culture. Nor is it unknow-
able to us except through the mists of legend. In the ever
deepening perspective of modern research, that age now

[7] See N. Glueck, "The Seventh Season of Archaeological Exploration in the
Negeb," *Bulletin of the American Schools of Oriental Research*, No. 152
(Dec. 1958), pp. 18 ff.

[8] See the report of G. Lankester Harding in the *Palestine Exploration
Quarterly*, Jan.-June, 1958, pp. 10-12.

stands in the full light of well documented historical day. Near Eastern kingdoms with magnificent cultural achievements had risen and fallen and Palestine itself had become the crossroads of Near Eastern trade long before Abraham arrived there. Indeed, the evidence shows that walled cities existed in Palestine as long before Abraham as Abraham lived before us!

It is not, however, the bare fact that advanced civilization existed in Canaan at 2000 B.C. that has been confirmed by archaeology. Rather, the closest correspondence in detail has been discovered between the setting of the lives of Abraham, Isaac, and Jacob as presented in Genesis and the particular Near Eastern social and political pattern of the Middle Bronze Age, during which the Bible locates the patriarchs. W. F. Albright acknowledges that "by and large there is astonishing similarity between the background provided by archaeology and that presupposed in Genesis."[9]

More specifically, the same writer has observed that excavations already conducted have demonstrated the existence during the Middle Bronze Age of practically every town mentioned in the patriarchal narratives; that there was in that age constant intercourse between Palestine and Egypt and, indeed, a general freedom of movement in the Near East, just as depicted in Genesis. Furthermore, the names of individual men and women found in the Biblical history of the patriarchs fit squarely with the collection of names gathered from sources from the first half of the second millennium B.C. and, moreover, not with the names of any later period.[10]

Various peoples mentioned in Genesis and once regarded as legendary by negative critics have been discovered by ar-

[9]Op. cit., p. 6.

[10]Similar confirmation is available for the names of Moses' time. For example, the names of both midwives in Exodus 1, Shiphrah and Puah, declared fictitious by some scholars, have been found as Northwest-Semitic women's names in the second millennium B.C.

chaeology to be the flesh and blood people the Bible indicates they were. The Hittites are a famous example; so too are the Horities, now identified with the Hurrians who played a vital role in Mesopotamian history in this period. And more recently still, mention of the Rephaim has been found in administrative texts from Canaan. The earliest non-Biblical reference to the covenant family continues to be the name of the people Israel on the thirteenth century stele of Pharaoh Merneptah of Egypt.

## Archaeological Support for Biblical Culture

The authenticity of the often strange social, legal, and economic practices attributed to the patriarchs in Genesis has also been corroborated. As is frequently the case, the light which archaeology throws on the sacred page is of even more interest in this area than its confirmation of Scripture.

The most helpful single site for the enlargement of our understanding of patriarchal culture has proved to be ancient Nuzu, situated east of the Tigris River. Excavations at the site were begun in 1925. Thousands of fifteenth century B.C. Babylonian legal documents were discovered there and the practices of Nuzu's Hurrian population which are disclosed therein are seen to be the framework of custom within which the Biblical patriarchs operated.[11] Although these documents come from a time several centuries after the patriarchs, the social practices they reflect are obviously older than the documents. Parallels found in old Babylonian texts from Ur attest to the existence of such practices in patriarchal times.

Elderly Nuzian couples without a male heir might adopt a man to manage their estate for them in their old age and he would become their heir, so preserving the family estate

[11]The Nuzu parallels were pointed out by C. H. Gordon in his article "Biblical Customs and the Nuzu Tablets," *Biblical Archaeologist*, III (1940), 1, pp. 1-12.

under the family name. That is what childless Abraham and Sarah did with Eliezer. The promise God afterward made to Abraham (cf. Gen. 15:4) reflects another stipulation of Nuzian adoption, that if a natural heir were born after the adoption, the natural heir had the right of precedence. Thus Isaac replaced Eliezer.

Similarly, it appears that when Jacob wandered north to Haran, Laban adopted him. There are adoption tablets where a daughter is given in marriage to the adopted son, as were Leah and Rachel to Jacob. Also in accordance with the rules of adoption, Laban insisted that since he was still alive, all the possessions of Jacob, the fugitive adopted heir, were still his (Laban's) (cf. Gen. 31:43).

Moreover, Rachel's theft of Laban's gods and Laban's anxiety to regain them ( cf. Gen. 31:19ff.) are explained by another feature of Nuzian adoption contracts. It was provided that these household gods, possession of which apparently guaranteed family headship, should go to a natural son subsequently born. By the time Jacob left Laban's household, we read of certain natural sons of Laban not mentioned at Jacob's arrival.

Other features of Nuzian legal procedure, such as the sale of birthright to one's brother, the unalterable validity of oral deathbed testaments (the oral blessing), the requirement in marriage contracts that a barren wife provide a handmaid for her husband to bear him children—all recall, illuminate, and confirm various incidents in Genesis.

From other ancient sites, such as Mari on the Middle Euphrates and Ugarit and Alalakh in Syria, comes similar information. Hittite sources, too, make an important contribution; and from them we take a final illustration concerning the background of the patriarchal narratives. Comparison of Hittite law with the account of Abraham's purchase of the field and cave of Machpelah from Ephron the Hittite shows that Genesis 23 benefits from a most intimate acquaintance with Hittite taxation technicalities in connection with the sale of real estate.[12] The bargaining, it turns out, revolved not around the price but around Abraham's unsuccessful effort to avoid purchasing the entire property unit, field as well as cave, which carried with it the burden of civil obligations. Such knowledge of Hittite legal subtleties is of particular significance for literary criticism, since these Hittite laws fell into oblivion about 1200 B.C.—long before the earliest of modern criticism's fictitious documentary sources of the Pentateuch.

## Archaeological Support for Biblical Records of the Days of Moses and Joshua

Leaving the patriarchs, what now is the witness of the ancient sites and sources to the historical accuracy of Biblical records of the Mosaic-Joshuan age, the age of exodus from Egypt and settlement in Canaan?

Archaeology speaks decisively against Wellhausen's notion that Pentateuchal legislation is too complex and its cultic provisions too elaborate for so early a time as that of Moses, to whom the authorship of the Pentateuch is attributed in both Old and New Testaments. As evidence of the antiquity of codified law, there are Assyrian and Hittite law codes from approximately the time of Moses, the Code of Hammurabi some three centuries before Moses, and the more recently discovered fragments of other Babylonian and Sumerian predecessors of Hammurabi's Code, dating back to Abraham's day.

Furthermore, the religious ritual required by the Pentateuchal laws is now seen to be similar in outward form to that in the cults of Israel's neighbors in the mid-second millennium B.C. The pattern of the tabernacle and its furnishings corresponds strikingly with that of contemporary non-

[12]This was first observed by M. R. Lehmann. Cf. "Abraham's Purchase of Machpelah and Hittite Law," *Bulletin of the American Schools of Oriental Research,* No. 129 (Feb. 1953), pp. 15 ff.

Israelite sanctuaries. There is, for example, the fourteenth century Canaanite temple uncovered at Hazor, with its court, main hall, and holy of holies. This sanctuary design is seen from excavations at Byblos to be at least as old as 2000 B.C.

A flood of new knowledge concerning Canaanite gods and ritual has flowed from the mound of the north Syrian seaport of Ras Shamra, anciently called Ugarit, where excavations were begun in 1929. Best known of the Ugaritic texts are the fourteenth century B.C. poetic legends and myths. There are also certain texts relating directly to cultic rites. Comparison of Ugaritic and Mosaic ritual reveals such similarities in terminology, sacrificial procedure, and sacred personnel as to render Wellhausen's viewpoint obsolete. Indeed, with the varieties of ceremonial symbolism found in the Mosaic legislation being traced in the pagan world to even pre-Mosaic times, the strategic situation in the modern debate is radically changing. The question of the historical genuineness of the Mosaic ceremonial system is yielding to the more basic question of the spiritual genuineness, that is, the divine origin, of the religion which the Mosaic ritual enshrined. It is becoming increasingly important to see clearly that the similarities of the Israelite worship to contemporary pagan worship are only on the superficial level of external forms and symbols. Israel's God was the Creator; Israel's neighbors worshiped idols. The Canaanites worshiped according to the dictates of their self-inflicted superstitions. Israel worshiped the living God according to a pattern actually made known by God to Moses on the mount. Archaeology, however, cannot bestow the heavenly gift of perception whereby a man recognizes the absolute uniqueness, the absolute authority and truthfulness of the revelation of God which came in and through the Mosaic sanctuary.

The story of the Israelite conquest of Canaan and settlement there can be read in the archaeological remains of the Late Bronze age (1500–1200 B.C.). Some historians, rejecting the Biblical representation, have suggested that Israel's settlement in Canaan came about by gradual infiltration and peaceful expansion. But the evidence of the repeated violent destruction of Canaanite cities during this period agrees well with the Biblical picture of a continuing work of conquest by Israel over a period of several generations, following the initial decisive campaigns of Joshua.

Incidentally, there is confirmation of the earlier (fourteenth century) date assigned to Joshua by the Biblical chronology in the discovery that sites like Bethel, Lachish, and Debir were destroyed by *fire* in the thirteenth century. For such destruction, being contrary to Joshua's regular policy not to destroy by fire,[13] must belong to a post-Joshuan phase of the Israelite conquest. Israel's settlement was chiefly in the central hill country of Canaan, and archaeological investigation has disclosed that that area had been wooded and only sparsely populated, but from about 1200 B.C. onward it became dotted with towns whose remains indicate a culture different from that of the surrounding Canaanites.

Many scholars have thought that in certain letters sent early in the fourteenth century by Canaanite city kings to Egyptian pharaohs and found at Tell el-Amarna in Egypt, there was a Canaanite version of the Biblical narrative of the Conquest. These Amarna letters refer to troubles in Canaan caused by the presence of Apiru (Habiru) warriors, whom many scholars identify with the Hebrews. The fact is that the Biblical and Amarna sources harmonize very well in such matters as the identity of the cities which the Canaanites lost in the early phases of the Conquest; but the Apiru activity referred to in the Amarna letters belongs to a time about a generation after Joshua and is to be related

[13]Apparently only Jericho and Ai among the southern cities were burned by Joshua and only Hazor in his northern campaign. See Joshua 11:13.

not to Israel's assault on Canaan but, it would seem, to the oppression of Israel by her Syrian neighbors.[14]

Our final archaeological illustration concerns the covenant pattern which according to the Pentateuchal records, God adopted in formalizing His relationship to Israel. Sinai is the scene of the ratification of the covenant. There God binds Israel in allegiance to Himself by oath and imposes His covenant law upon them. Recent studies[15] have revealed how remarkably similar the formal proceedings at Sinai were to the standard procedure followed in international diplomacy of the second millennium B.C. for solemnizing treaties with vassals as is seen in texts of Hittite covenants.

The parallels embrace the ceremony of ratification and the contents (even the very outline) of the covenant document. Like the Biblical Decalogue (Exod. 20:1 ff.), ancient vassal treaties began with a preamble identifying the lord of the covenant and a historical prologue recalling his previous benefits to the vassal or dependent prince, and then moved on to the particular obligations imposed upon the vassal. Prominent also in both Biblical and Hittite covenants were the invocation of witnesses, the proclaiming of the curses and blessings of the covenant, and the requirement that the covenant document be deposited in a sanctuary and periodically read to the vassal people. The genuine historical ring of the Biblical narrative and legislation should be clear to all.

A further principle in the administration of vassal treaties was that they were renewed from time to time, as when the covenant lord's death seemed near and he desired to confirm the dynastic succession of his son. The subject people was then required to take an oath of allegiance to the royal

---

[14]Judges 3:8 ff. See the author's articles on "The Ha-BI-ru—Kin or Foe of Israel?" *Westminster Theological Journal*, XIX (Nov. 1956) 1, pp. 1 ff.; XIX (May, 1957), 2, pp. 170 ff.; XX (Nov. 1957), 1, pp. 46 ff.

[15]See especially G. E. Mendenhall, *Law and Covenant in Israel and the Ancient Near East, The Biblical Colloquium,* 1955.

heir and a new covenant document was prepared, the old historical prologue and the stipulations being brought up to date.

It is clear that the book of Deuteronomy is precisely such a document. With the death of Moses imminent, it was necessary to renew the covenant with the new generation from the wilderness, confronting them with the demand to pledge their obedience to Joshua, the divinely appointed successor to Moses. Examination shows that the structure of Deuteronomy follows precisely the pattern of the ancient vassal treaties. The critical importance of this is that the whole Wellhausen scheme rested on the dating of Deuteronomy in the seventh century B.C. For rationalistic higher critics to continue to accept that untenable date must strike men who are concerned to do justice to all the facts as obscurantism. In continuing to hold the late date, the critics ignore the decisive evidence of the Hittite treaties for the authenticity of Deuteronomy as a product of the Mosaic age.

Archaeological research has, of course, also posed some new problems with respect to the accuracy of Biblical history in points of detail. But this need cause no undue concern for the Bible student. On the Biblical side, allowance must be made for various possibilities of interpretation and, as we have seen, for a measure of textual variation. On the archaeological side, allowance must be made for the fragmentary nature of the evidence (only a few score of some 25,000 sites in Biblical lands have been excavated) and for the differences and uncertainties in the interpretation of the evidence available, due in part to the relative youth of this science.

Those who recognize the Word of God for what it is can with the patience of faith await the final vindication of the perfect truthfulness of that Word. Those who lack such perception will meanwhile continue to sing the favorite hymn of the critical cult, "It Ain't Necessarily So," seizing upon the apparent conflicts in detail between archaeological data and the Biblical history as an excuse. Nevertheless, every generation of negative critics will find itself in perpetual strategic retreat, as advancing archaeology relentlessly contradicts the examples of alleged Biblical error most confidently publicized by their fathers. It is not, however, the ever increasing witness of archaeology but the self-witness of the divine Word which leaves all negative criticism of that Word without acceptable excuse in the sight of its Author.

*Chapter 8*

# IS THE TEXT OF
# THE NEW TESTAMENT
# RELIABLE?

*by*

A. BERKELEY MICKELSEN

## Chapter 8

# IS THE TEXT OF THE NEW TESTAMENT RELIABLE?

AFTER THE GOSPELS, epistles, and the book of Revelation were written, they were read and circulated among particular groups in the early church. Therefore we naturally ask, How were the contents of the New Testament transmitted to us, and how can we be sure that the original writings of these Gospels and letters were not substantially altered in the process of being handed down to us?

Thanks to the painstaking work of scholars during the last four hundred years, this question can be answered with confidence. Although they have found that many changes have occurred in the copying of the manuscripts, they have shown that most of these are insignificant indeed. By following certain basic principles of textual criticism, scholars have been able to recover in most instances the wording of the original writing.

### Writing and Writing Material

The New Testament was written in Greek. The Greek language has both capital and small letters. The Greeks of the first century usually printed their letters, but sometimes they wrote them in longhand as we do. Printing in capital letters without any space between words and without punctuation was the most common method of writing in ancient times. We find they simply wrote line after line of printed letters.

Those who copied the writings of the New Testament up to the time of the invention of the printing press followed a general pattern. The manuscripts from the third to the tenth centuries A.D. were copied in capitals. (The papyrus materials before the third century are also in capitals.) These are technically referred to as *uncials*. The manuscripts copied from the ninth to the sixteenth centuries were written in small letters and with a flowing hand. These are referred to as *cursives*. Abbreviations for *God, Jesus, Lord, man, father*, and *Spirit* were often employed.

The material used for writing is most interesting. Paper did not come into use until the thirteenth century A.D. In ancient times broken pieces of pottery were used for "scratch paper." These are called *ostraca*.

The material used for most letters, contracts, or any extensive writing in New Testament times was made from the papyrus reed. This grew in the marshes of Egypt. The core or piths of these reeds were cut into strips and laid across each other at right angles to form sheets. When the strips were pressed and pasted together, they made excellent writing "paper." Usually these small papyrus sheets were then pasted together to make longer sheets which were rolled up into scrolls. Only rarely was the codex or book form employed. Egypt exported papyrus throughout the Mediterranean world.

The original writings of the New Testament were probably on papyrus. These were read and copied until they became worn out. Undoubtedly the worn originals were preserved as long as possible. But after a while the climate in which they were located brought about their disintegration. The early copies of the originals were also made on papyrus. It was the most frequently used material for New Testament manuscripts until the beginning of the fourth century.

From the fourth to the thirteenth centuries parchment was used. This consisted of the skins of sheep, lambs, goats, or calves prepared for writing. This material was much more durable than papyrus, and is the material used in most of the New Testament manuscripts from which modern texts are drawn.

From the thirteenth century on paper began to compete with parchment. With the coming of the printing press, paper was victorious and parchment became one of the curios of a bygone literary era.

### Quantity of Materials Transmitted

How valuable is the New Testament? We can hardly find words to answer. Through its pages men have come to know God in Jesus Christ. To each believer the New Testament has a limitless value. That this has been true throughout the centuries is shown by the abundance of manuscripts we have of the New Testament. By the middle of the twentieth century, there were nearly 4,500 known Greek manuscripts.

In contrast to this number, there are very few manuscripts of the classics of antiquity. F. F. Bruce points out that there are only nine or ten good manuscripts of Caesar's *Gallic War* (written between 58-50 B.C.). The oldest of these manuscripts was written some nine hundred years after Caesar's day. The history by Thucydides (c. 460-400 B.C.), the famous Greek historian, has come down to us from only eight manuscripts, and a few papyrus scraps[1] written around the beginning of the Christian era. The earliest of the existing manuscripts comes from about A.D. 900. This means there were thirteen hundred years between the time Thucydides wrote and the earliest copy of what he wrote. Yet historians and classical scholars regard Thucydides as a first-class historian. They are sure they know his approach to history and what his distinct emphases were.

No such gap exists between the manuscripts of the New

[1] F. F. Bruce, *Are the New Testament Documents Reliable?* (Grand Rapids: Wm. B. Eerdmans Publishing Co., 1954), pp. 20-21.

Testament and the original writings. Two of the important uncial manuscripts, called B and Aleph, are from the fourth century A.D. Three of the Chester Beatty papyri contain most of the New Testament writings: (1) the four Gospels and Acts; (2) nine of Paul's letters with Hebrews. These two came from A.D. 200-250. (3) P[47], which contains Revelation 9-17, belongs to A.D. 250-300. The earliest scrap of the New Testament which we possess is P[52]. It contains five verses of John (18:31-33, 37, 38). This papyrus fragment is now in the John Rylands Library in Manchester, England. Deissmann and others have dated this scrap in the reign of Hadrian (A.D. 117-138). Here then is a papyrus fragment which comes from approximately A.D. 125. Since the traditional date for the fourth Gospel is between A.D. 90 and 100, this particular papyrus copy was circulating within thirty-five to forty years of the time the Gospel was written.[2]

The Greek manuscripts extend all the way from this earliest fragment to the time of the printing press. From then on, of course, the text was printed in Greek instead of being handwritten.

Not only are there Greek manuscripts in large numbers, but also thousands of manuscripts in languages which were translated from Greek or Latin. These are known as versions. It is very convenient to divide these geographically as far as the Mediterranean area is concerned. Some were produced in the East including Egypt, and others were produced in the West. Metzger includes in the Eastern group: Syriac, Coptic (Egyptian versions), Armenian, Georgian, Ethiopic, Arabic, Sogdian, and Nubian. In the Western group he puts the Latin, Gothic, Old Slavic, Frankish, and Anglo-Saxon versions.[3] Three of these are, on the whole, of

---

[2]cf. *Ibid.*, pp. 21, 22.

[3]Bruce Metzger, "The Evidence of the Versions for the Text of the New Testament," *New Testament Manuscript Studies.* The Materials and the Making of a Critical Apparatus. Editors, Merrill M. Parvis and Allen P. Wikgren (Chicago: The University of Chicago Press, 1950), pp. 26, 27.

great importance: the Syriac versions, the Egyptian or Coptic versions, and the Latin versions.

Syriac was spoken in Syria and Mesopotamia. It is very similar to the Aramaic spoken by Christ and the apostles in Palestine. This means it belongs to the Semitic family of languages and is directly related to Biblical Hebrew. The various translations into Syriac came from the second to the sixth centuries A.D. The Old Syriac, the Peshitta Syriac and the Philoxenian or Harkleian Syriac represent various types of the most important Syriac translations.

The Egyptian or Coptic versions consist of a half-dozen or more varieties of the Old Egyptian tongue. Sahidic was the dialect of upper Egypt, Bohairic of lower Egypt. Between these two extremes were intermediate dialects, such as Fayumic, Memphitic, Achmimic, and sub-Achmimic. Is it not significant that every dialect group of people wanted the New Testament in their particular dialect?

In a similar way there are several Latin versions or translations. The Old Latin seems to be divided into two parts —the African Latin and the European Latin (the Latin of Italy, southern France etc.). St. Jerome, the translator of the famous Vulgate, completed the Gospels in A.D. 384 and the rest of the Testament by about 390. For a while the Old Latin and the Vulgate were both in use, but the Vulgate soon gained a superior position. It was not until the ninth century, however, that the Vulgate was assured of being the Latin text used by all. It became the official text of the Roman Catholic Church at the Council of Trent in 1546.

All these versions are important because they originally were derived from a very early Greek text. The Old Syriac and Old Latin were translated about A.D. 150. The earliest Egyptian translation was made about A.D. 200. If a scholar could get the original form of the Old Latin, for example, this would give him a helpful picture of the Greek text from which the Old Latin was translated. However, the versions were copied and recopied. In the process of being copied, changes (additions, subtractions, alterations) were made. Thus scholars working on a version must strive to uncover the original text of the version. To the extent that this can be done, the version contributes valuable data about the Greek text from which it was translated.

The New Testament has also been partially preserved in the quotations made by the early Church Fathers. Some of their writings, like First Clement, contain many extensive quotations from both the Old and New Testaments. At times a Church Father would quote very carefully; other times he obviously quoted more loosely from memory. Also, the text of the Father has been changed in the process of being copied. Therefore each Father and quotation must be evaluated independently. But with careful evaluation the form of the text quoted by the Father can give helpful information about the New Testament text which he knew.

There is one more group of materials in which the text of the New Testament has been preserved. The manuscripts of this group are called lectionaries. They consist of reading lessons used in the public services of the church. By the middle of the twentieth century more than sixteen hundred of these reading lessons had been classified (given a number: *1*, 1; *1*, 2, etc.

There are lectionaries of the Gospels and lectionaries of the Acts and the epistles. In the Gospel lectionaries passages were selected from the Gospels to be read in the particular order demanded by a liturgical calendar. The series of readings actually covered the content of the Gospels. A regular formula was used to introduce the section to be read, and often a formula closed the reading. In introducing a teaching section, we might find: "The Lord said to His disciples." A favorite concluding formula was: "Let him who has ears, be sure to listen!"[4] These lectionaries appear from the sixth century on. Although they are not early, the text which they quote may itself be early and of a high quality. Being preserved in a form where it was read, it tended never to be altered.

What a quantity of material! There are thousands of Greek manuscripts, a great quantity of material in the various versions, many quotations from the New Testament to be found in the writings of the Church Fathers, and a sizable quantity of material to be found in the lectionaries. When properly evaluated, all of these help the scholar to recover what the original author actually wrote.

### Quality of the Material Transmitted

One thing should be clear. Since so many people worked at copying the New Testament writings, thousands of changes were made in the process. How many alterations were made in all the Greek manuscripts, we do not know. The number may be as high as 150,000. Most of these are insignificant, however. A scribe may have left out a "the." He may have changed a present tense to an imperfect tense. He may have used a different grammatical construction from the one the author had. Such changes rarely alter the meaning.

The changes which scribes made are usually divided into two categories: unintentional alterations and intentional alterations. The unintentional kind involve errors of *the eye* as the scribe was copying. He was copying a line which had no word divisions and no punctuation. He may have confused letters which were very similar. He may have omitted similar words or clauses which follow one another. He may have written a word twice. Alteration could also have oc-

[4]Ernest Cadman Colwell, "The Contents of the Gospel Lectionary," *Prolegomena to the Study of the Lectionary Text of the Gospels.* Editors, Ernest Cadman Colwell and Donald W. Riddle (Chicago: The University of Chicago Press, 1933), pp. 1, 2.

curred in errors of *the ear*. If one scribe were dictating to another, the sound of the short "i," the short "e," and the long "e," may have been slurred, so that the scribe wrote one letter instead of the other.

Then there were errors of *memory* in which the scribe instead of writing one word for "knowledge" wrote a synonym or a compound of the same word. Further, there were errors of *judgment*. Sometimes a scribe may have written a note of explanation of a verse in the margin. The next scribe to copy this may have added the note to the text, thinking that these comments were something the earlier scribe had accidentally omitted when he was copying. These are called "marginal glosses."

Finally, errors arose from *the language habits* of the scribe himself. Early scribes having Greek as their native tongue occasionally reproduced their own speech habits. They would express the thought they found in Scripture in the way they would say it, rather than in the exact words of the original author.

The intentional changes usually were made with the best of motives. The scribes wanted to improve the writing, make it smoother and clearer. This attitude led to a number of stylistic and grammatical changes. Other times the scribes tried to make the writing more precise. In Mark 1:1, 2, the evangelist Mark wrote: "just as it has been written in Isaiah the prophet."[5] Since half of Mark's quotation comes from Malachi and the other half from Isaiah, the scribes altered what Mark wrote and substituted: "just as it has been written in the prophets."

There are also many assimilations in the Gospels. This means that the copying scribe remembered the wording of one Gospel and so he "corrected" another Gospel to make it similar. For example, in Matthew 12:46-50 we have the ac-

[5]This and a number of other passages quoted in this chapter appear as the author's own translation.

count of Christ's mother and brothers who came to speak to Him and could not because of the crowd. In verse 46 Matthew tells of the endeavors of Christ's mother and brothers. Then in verse 48 Jesus replies to the one who told Him about the presence of His kin: "'Who is my mother? and who are my brethren?" However, verse 47 appears not to have been written by Matthew but by a scribe who was acquainted with the account of Luke 8:20. Luke wrote: "And it was reported to him: 'Your mother and your brothers stand outside wishing to see you.' " Hence in Matthew 12:47 (this verse is bracketed in Nestle's Greek text; RSV puts it in the margin) one finds: "And a certain one said to him: 'Your mother and your brothers stand outside seeking to speak to you.' " A change like this is perfectly harmless. To decide that this is an alteration, a scholar must examine and compare all other manuscripts as well as the flow of thought in the particular passage.

Sometimes changes were made in the interest of doctrinal matters (see I John 5:7, 8 in King James Version; then read this passage in the ASV). Liturgical additions are also found. An example of this is to be noted in the conclusion of the Lord's prayer. "For thine is the kingdom, and the power, and the glory, forever. Amen" (Matt. 6:13). This entire verse now appears to have been an addition for the sake of its liturgical value. Changes representing the scribe's way of life are found. To the disciples who wondered why they could not cast out a demon, Christ replied: "This kind is not able to go out except by prayer" (Mark 9:29). An early scribe added: "and fasting." In his way of life, prayer and fasting were complementary. So for him this was a natural part of Christ's command.

No one should be disturbed by these changes. Since the time of the Reformation great numbers of additional early manuscripts have been found, and a sound method of evaluating all the textual materials has been developed. From

1500 to 1800 "the textus receptus" or "the received text" held sway. It was from this text that the King James Version was translated. This text is one which has been made smooth with additions, etc. It shows the many changes which were made throughout the centuries.

CLASSIFICATION OF MANUSCRIPTS

From 1800 to the present time scholars have been perfecting a method of classifying manuscripts in terms of groups or families. In such classification one of the basic principles is to group manuscripts having a number of readings in common as coming from the same geographical area. Hence scholars have worked both on the characteristics of individual manuscripts and those of groups of manuscripts. Characteristics were tied to manuscripts and families which were thought to have come from the same geographical area. After labels became attached to groups or families, further investigations have occasionally indicated a need for altering some of the earlier opinions about these families of manuscripts. Yet the classification and the characteristics of the family are very important to the scholar in his attempt to get back to the original text. Here are the family classifications used by a majority of textual scholars today.

(1) The Byzantine text or family. This text may have originated in the fourth century. It grew in prominence and by the eighth century it was used almost everywhere in the Greek world. It is a smooth, rounded-out text. This smoothness probably was achieved by editing on the part of scribes over a period of time and then was preserved in this particular form. This textual family is regarded as a base for judging whether manuscripts are early or late. Late manuscripts tend to agree with the Byzantine text; early ones show distinct differences from it.

(2) The Alexandrian text or family. This seems to have originated in Alexandria, and it is regarded as an early text.

Though some changes have been made, the scribes who copied these manuscripts have stuck closely to what they received without extensive additions or alterations. Such scholars as Westcott and Hort called this a "neutral text" and prized it very highly. Such terminology has a bad connotation. Even if the family as a whole were "neutral" in the way it copied and preserved the text, this would not make it true of all the individual readings. The readings of manuscripts from this family are taken very seriously by scholars who want evidence for establishing the exact language of Mark or Paul.

(3) The Western text or family. This family is confined to those manuscripts which are geographically western, that is, from the western part of the Mediterranean. Certain texts —D for example—are bilingual, having both Greek and Latin. These belong in the Western family as does the Old Latin version, as well as quotations from a number of the early Church Fathers. While the Western text certainly is early, one of its main characteristics is that of additions. All the way through the book of Acts manuscript D and its allies contain additional material which the other families do not have. In a situation like this textual criticism can record the fact of these additions, but the reason for such additions is not at all clear.

(4) The Caesarean text or family. This is one of the newer families to be discovered. How much unity the family has is not clear. The term *Caesarean* indicates the use of this text in the area of Caesarea, although it seems clear that it also was used elsewhere. Some scholars think that this family stands between the Alexandrian and the Western. In this case, it could be a mere mixture rather than a distinct family with distinct characteristics.

(5) The Eastern text or family. This consists of the Old Syriac version and the quotations which agree with this

type of text. It is an early text which comes from the eastern end of the Mediterranean.

These families or text types do not consist of fixed categories. It is by distinctive traits that a manuscript is put into one category or another. Labels and categories change, but the characteristics abide. Therefore classification of manuscripts on the basis of their characteristics helps the scholar to know whether a particular reading is supported by manuscripts which have a text that gives evidence of being both early and substantially unchanged from the original.

### Evaluation of Divergent Readings

When a scholar is faced with two different readings, he must weigh carefully both the external and internal evidence. The external evidence refers to the Greek manuscripts, versions, Church Fathers and lectionaries which support each reading. The internal evidence refers to how well each reading fits into the train of thought being pursued by the writer. Here the scholar must consider whether either of the readings reflects scribal alteration. The investigator must also be alert to see whether one reading may be foreign to the thought of the writer. Here are the main principles which textual scholars follow.[6]

### Specific Criteria for Genuineness

(1) *The age of the text* of a manuscript is more significant *than the age of the manuscript* itself.

(2) Readings supported *by ancient witnesses*, however, especially *from different groups*, are generally preferable.

(3) The reconstruction of *the history of a variant* is basic to judgment about it.

---

[6]Professor Wikgren has an excellent summary of these in Ira M. Price, *Ancestry of our English Bible*, edited and revised by William A. Irwin and Allen P. Wikgren (second revised edition; New York: Harper and Brothers, 1949), pp. 220-222.

(4) The *quality rather than quantity* of witnesses is more important in determining a reading.

(5) *Identity of readings,* particularly in errors, *implies identity of origin.*

(6) The *shorter reading* is generally preferable.

(7) The *more difficult reading* is generally preferable.

The reason the shorter and more difficult readings are generally preferable is that scribes were tempted to enlarge for the sake of clarification rather than to make a statement more concise. Also scribes tended to make difficult readings easier rather than to make something harder which was stated in a simple, straightforward manner. If either of the last two principles is overworked, such a course can only lead to absurdities being accepted. But kept in proper bounds, these principles are very useful.

### Specific Indications of Alteration

(1) Readings which bear the earmarks of *stylistic or grammatical improvement* are suspect.

(2) Readings which bear the earmarks of *doctrinal controversy* occurring in the time of the scribe are suspect.

(3) Variants combining *the appearance of improvement with the absence of its reality* are suspect.

### General Criteria for Genuineness

(1) The reading is preferred *which best suits the author's characteristic tendencies.*

(2) The reading is preferred *which best suits the context* and *which best explains the origin of the other variant or variants.*

The last two criteria are certainly those given careful attention today. In Mark 1:1 there is a question as to whether the phrase "the Son of God" was part of Mark's original text. The external manuscript evidence is rather evenly divided. The decision must be based upon this external evi-

dence, these general criteria for genuineness, and the possibility of a scribal omission. These last two words "Son of
God" (two words in Greek) have the same case endings and
form (last two letters) as Jesus Christ, the two preceding
words. Vincent Taylor believes there are strong reasons for
accepting the phrase as original. He points to Mark's use
of the phrase "the Son of God" in 3:11; 5:7; 15:39. "My beloved Son" is found in 1:11; 9:7; "the son of the Blessed"
occurs in 14:61.[7] Agreeing with Vincent Taylor in his reasoning, the writer would add that the external evidence in favor
of the phrase "Son of God" comes from the Alexandrian, Western, and Byzantine families. Likewise the versional evidence
is excellent. Agreement among such a diversity of witnesses
cannot be easily dismissed.

## Significance of Textual Criticism

The type of careful procedure which has just been outlined should remove any fear that we do not know what is
the true text of the New Testament. The general integrity
of the New Testament is beyond dispute. Allen Paul Wikgren, an outstanding authority in the area of text, concludes:
"Only 400 or so of the 150,000 variants materially affect the
sense, and of these perhaps fifty are of real significance. But
no essential teaching of the New Testament is greatly
affected by them."[8]

The tremendous amount of labor put into the study of the
text of the New Testament is an indirect testimony to its
greatness. Further, the job is not complete. More manuscripts will be discovered. Better critical texts will appear.
An easier and clearer format will be worked out to see what
witnesses are most important.

All these things increase our responsibility to make full use

[7]For a good picture of how external and internal evidence is evaluated,
see Vincent Taylor, *The Gospel According to Mark* (London: Macmillan
and Co., 1957), p. 152.

[8]Price, edited and revised by Irwin and Wikgren, p. 222.

of this treasure which has come down to us. Men have given up their lives rather than hand over the Scriptures to the persecutor. Throughout the ages men have spent their lives in copying and preserving as well as interpreting the Scriptures. Modern scholars have made full use of all modern mechanical aids to photograph and process manuscripts and their variants. How tragic if we merely conclude that the New Testament is the best attested-to piece of ancient literature and that we can be confident that we know what the original authors wrote. This is all true, but far more important is the fact that the central Person in the New Testament proclaimed good news. As the servants of the Pharisees testified: "Never did a man speak in this fashion as this man speaks" (John 7:46). Or as the Saviour Himself said: "The words which I have spoken are Spirit kind of words and are life" (John 6:63). These words are ours, indeed, to make our very own and to make them known to others.

*Chapter 9*

# IS THE NEW TESTAMENT HISTORICALLY ACCURATE?

*by*

Robert H. Mounce

*Chapter 9*

# IS THE NEW TESTAMENT
# HISTORICALLY ACCURATE?

How IMPORTANT IS IT that the New Testament be accurate in all its many details? Wouldn't that be asking too much of a book that doesn't pretend to be a textbook in such areas as geography or science? How could we expect perfect accuracy on the part of those hundreds of scribes who copied and recopied the books of the New Testament, from the time they were written down until the invention of printing in the fifteenth century? And in fact isn't the Bible full of little minor contradictions? For example, where *was* Jesus when He preached the Sermon on the Mount? Matthew says that He "went up on the mountain" (Matt. 5:1), and Luke says that He had just come down and "stood on a level place" (Luke 6:17). Does it really make any difference? In either case we still have His marvelous teaching and that is what is really important!

And so the argument goes. Sounds convincing doesn't it? However, those who reason in this way have overlooked one basic point. Christianity, unlike other religions, is not simply a code of ethics or a new scheme of morality. It is what the theologians call a historical religion. It cannot be considered apart from the historical traditions associated with its origin, but is inseparably entwined with history itself. Its message is not "good conduct," but "good news"—that's what the word *gospel* means. This good news is about something that happened in a certain place at a certain time.

So you see it *is* important whether we can trust the New Testament when it tells us about something that happened. The Gospel writer is either right or wrong. If he is wrong in an area where we can check him (history), how can we rely upon his accuracy in an area where no checks are possible (doctrine)? The whole thing stands or falls together. F. F. Bruce, the Scottish New Testament scholar whose works are so widely read in both the conservative and liberal camps, has rightly said that the "historical 'once-for-all-ness' of Christianity . . . makes the reliability of the writings which purport to record this revelation a question of first-rate importance" (*Are the New Testament Documents Reliable?* p. 12).

About the middle of the last century there arose an influential school of thought which has become known as the Tübingen school (after the University of Tübingen in southwest Germany). For reasons which are now largely discredited, this group of men decided that many of the books of the New Testament were not written by the traditional authors but by men of the second century who arbitrarily altered the historical origins of Christianity in such a way as to correspond with the developing thought of the postapostolic church. F. C. Baur, the spokesman for this Hegelian reinterpretation of Christianity, held that of all Paul's epistles, only Galatians, I and II Corinthians, and Romans 1-14 could be accepted as genuine.

Among the books judged to be second-century fabrications, and therefore not reliable, were the four Gospels and Acts. In other words, the history of early Christianity was placed under suspicion. Now, the further the recording of an event is separated from the event itself, the stronger the case for the intrusion of error. For example, if the exploits of the pony express, which for one short year about a century ago galloped the mail from St. Joe to Sacramento, were written down today for the first time, we would have plenty of reason to doubt the accuracy of the account. Memories grow dim and imaginations run wild. Yet this one hundred year lapse is about the same span of time as was supposed to have existed between the events in Acts and their recording by "Luke." The natural result of this critical frame of mind was to place the entire New Testament under suspicion and those holding such a viewpoint often grasped with glee any apparent historical inaccuracy which would feed their bias.

HISTORICAL PROBABILITY OF A RELIABLE RECORD

It is not our purpose to handle the question philosophically, but let's take time to consider briefly the historical *probability* that in the New Testament we have a reliable record. When we look at the textual evidence for secular works of antiquity we are surprised to find only a moderate number of copies, almost all of which are quite late. Caesar's famous *Gallic War*, written about a half century before Christ, can boast of only nine or ten good copies and the oldest of these comes from the ninth century A.D. Our earliest manuscript of the *History of Thucydides* is over thirteen hundred years later than the original.

On the other hand, when we look at the evidence for the New Testament we learn that there are in existence more than 4,000 Greek manuscripts (or portions thereof), some of which are very early. One of these goes back almost to the event itself. In addition, there are second-century translations, such as the Old Syriac and the Old Latin, and writings of the early Church Fathers who quote at length portions of the New Testament.

The two most famous manuscripts are the Codex Vaticanus in Rome and the Codex Sinaiticus in the British Museum. These beautifully preserved manuscripts (the writing is as clear and understandable as a first grade primer) date from about the middle of the fourth century. The important Chester Beatty papyri go back another hundred years. The Egerton papyrus, evidently a manual designed to teach converts the gospel stories, is dated 150, and the famous Rylands fragment is part of the Gospel of John which was circulating in Egypt within forty years of the time the beloved disciple signed his name to the original.

From the standpoint of literary evidence the only logical conclusion is that the case for the reliability of the New Testament is infinitely stronger than that for any other record of antiquity.

But what about the all-important question of the gap between an event and its initial recording? Here archaeology has something of significance to say. Dr. Millar Burrows of Yale has pointed out that the study of historical grammar based on archaeological evidence shows that the Greek of the New Testament is first century Greek, leading to the conclusion that the New Testament books were written during the first century. He holds further that the hypothesis of a deliberate and remarkably successful use of archaic language (by a later writer)—the only other alternative in view of the nature of the Greek of the New Testament—is "wholly improbable."[1] The excessive skepticism of many liberal theologians stems not from a careful evaluation of the available data, but from an enormous predisposition against the supernatural.

We must also add a word about just what constitutes a historical error or discrepancy in the Biblical text. A. A. Hodge, a famous theologian who taught at Princeton, defined a discrepancy as a statement in the original text designed to set forth as true that which is absolutely contradictory to other statements in the original text or to definitely

[1]Millar Burrows, *What Mean These Stones?* (New Haven: American Schools of Oriental Research, 1941), pp. 53, 54.

ascertained elements of human knowledge.[2] In other words, *proving* the existence of a contradiction is not as easy as one might imagine. First of all, the "erroneous statement" must be shown to be in the original text; then that the secular record was incontestably correct; and finally that the two are *essentially incapable* of being harmonized. To chat about "contradictions" is one thing; to prove them is something else.

One of the intriguing things about the Bible is that nowhere does it make an attempt to gloss over what might appear on the surface to be a contradiction. For example, Luke says that Jesus met and healed blind Bartimaeus as He drew near to Jericho (Luke 18:35), while Mark says that it was as He was leaving Jericho (Mark 10:46). Matthew agrees with Mark as to the location ("as they went out from Jericho"—Matt. 20:29 ASV), but he mentions two blind men instead of one (Matt. 20:30). If three of us were writing parallel accounts of something which we wanted our friends to accept as absolutely true, we might be a bit more careful about the details. However, when such "contradictions" are studied, they inevitably have a way of resolving themselves, or at least pointing out a possible avenue of explanation.[3] In the past half century or so archaeology has again and again turned up an inscription or some other artifact which has solved one "contradiction" after another. Just because all the answers are not now available does not mean that the problems are incapable of being solved. Patience! God is in no hurry, and something has to be left to faith.

One reason for these problems is that the Bible is the most complex literary unity known to man. It was written by about forty authors, and these from every strata of society.

[2]A. A. Hodge, *Outlines of Theology* (New York: A. C. Armstrong and Son, 1908), pp. 75, 76.

[3]For example, it has been suggested that in Jesus' day there possibly were an old and a new Jericho a short distance apart. Matthew and Mark could have viewed the miracle as occurring when Jesus left the one, and Luke, as the Lord was about to enter the other.

It contains every conceivable literary form and was more than fifteen hundred years in the making. Apparent discrepancies are what we would expect. Any telltale signs of clever editing would simply weaken the case for authenticity.

But enough of this philosophical ground work. Let's look at the text itself in the light of archaeology and historical research.

### *Luke the Historian*

Besides being a physician (Col. 4:14) and Paul's traveling companion, Luke was the historian of primitive Christianity. The two New Testament books which came from his pen (the third Gospel and Acts) are in reality two parts of one great work. (One papyrus roll could not accommodate both halves.) They tell of the origin of Christianity and its major missionary expansion in the ministry of the Apostle Paul.

In the Prologue (Luke 1:1-4) Luke sets down the occasion for his work, calls attention to the reliability of his sources, indicates his own qualifications, and states his purpose. Then, continuing as a good historian, he starts his narrative by sketching the historical context: "There was in the days of Herod, king of Judea, a certain priest named Zacharias, of the course of Abijah. . . ." As Luke unfolds his story we are introduced to a whole array of historical personages, both Roman and Jewish, secular and religious. Note the meticulous concern for detail in his preface to the account of John the Baptist:

> Now in the fifteenth year of the reign of Tiberius Caesar, Pontius Pilate being governor of Judea, and Herod being tetrarch of Galilee, and his brother Philip tetrarch of the region of Ituraea and Trachonitis, and Lysanias tetrarch of Abilene, in the high-priesthood of Annas and Caiaphas, the word of God came unto John the son of Zacharias (Luke 3:1, 2 ASV).

Now any writer who goes to such length to root his narrative in the historical setting is simply inviting the critic to examine the accuracy of his record. How different from this is the story of the birth of Lao-tzu, the founder of Taoism. This one is said to have been born a fully matured "wise old philosopher" with white hair, having been carried in his mother's womb for over seventy years! Or compare the historicity of Christianity with the gradual and complex emergence of Hinduism, which has developed at least six different types of religion, each embodied in successive sets of documents. The Christian faith did not rise from a spiritist's seance or the misty regions of pre-historic legend. It took place *in time* and invites us to check up on it if we so desire.

A good indication of an ancient historian's reliability is the liberty he allows himself in the matter of reporting speeches. Here is an opportunity for him to display all his dramatic and literary skill. One such example is the eloquent oration which Josephus places upon the lips of Abraham as he stands with dagger poised over his beloved Isaac. If the aged patriarch could hear what he is supposed to have said, he would be completely dumfounded. But what do we find when we turn to the early speeches of Peter as they are recorded in Acts? (These, of course, are just summaries of what was said and not verbatim reports.) Far from being "exhibit A" of Luke's literary ability, they are written in a style of Greek which is quite often awkward and at times almost untranslatable. Since Luke normally wrote as good Greek as can be found in the New Testament, what can be said about this lapse into mediocrity? Experts in Aramaic, the language spoken throughout the eastern Mediterranean in the days of Jesus, have demonstrated that these speeches, when translated back into Aramaic, have a way of smoothing out and becoming perfectly understandable. This means that their awkwardness in Greek is the result of a rather literal translation from the original Aramaic. Quite possibly a written document was involved. This reluctance of Luke to tamper with his sources is a significant indication of his careful concern to report as nearly as possible exactly what took place.

Our confidence in Luke as a historian is strengthened even more when we compare his writings with the results of modern archaeology. In what is perhaps the severest test of the accuracy of an ancient historian—correctly designating the host of public officials which enter his narrative—Luke comes through with flying colors. What makes this so difficult is that Rome allowed her various provinces to carry on (as far as could be safely allowed) their traditional forms of government. To handle with precision the bewildering array of official titles in each locality was no task for a person unconcerned with precision. The writer of Acts never falters in this crucial test, a remarkable feat for even a first-century historian to say nothing of a second century fabricator.

Luke correctly refers to the governor of Cyprus as a *proconsul* (Acts 13:7, Greek). Since Cyprus became a Senatorial province in 22 B.C. it would be governed no longer by an Imperial *legatus* but by a *proconsul* as Luke indicates. Achaia was also a Senatorial province and Luke's reference to Gallio as a *proconsul* (Acts 18:12 ASV) is confirmed by the famous Delphi inscription which reads in part: "As Lucius Junius Gallio, my friend, and the *proconsul* of Achaia wrote. . . ." The civic authorities at Thessalonica are called *politarchs* (Acts 17:6, 8, Greek). Since this title was unknown in classical literature, it was immediately assumed by the critics that Luke had committed another *faux pas*. However, archaeology has now uncovered some nineteen inscriptions from this period in which the rulers of Macedonian cities (and Thessalonica is the city in question in five of these) are called *politarchs*. (Cf. F. F. Bruce's excellent article in *Revelation and the Bible*, pp. 319-331.)

Again, Luke refers to the local officials at Philippi as *praetors*. Since Philippi was a Roman colony, the official title of these men would be *duumvir,* but here again Luke has made no mistake. The more imposing title of *praetor,* we have learned, was a courtesy granted to rulers of Roman colonies, and hence to the civic magistrates at Philippi.

In Acts 28:7 Luke refers to the governor of Malta by the curious title, "the first man of the island." But now inscriptions have been found both in Greek and Latin indicating that this was in fact the proper designation for rulers of that island. Luke speaks of *tetrarchs, lictors, Asiarchs,* and in one place (Acts 28:16) of a *stratopedarch* (identified as the commander of the Imperial couriers), all with unfailing accuracy.

When the narrative in Acts is subjected to this searching test for historical accuracy and comes through with a perfect score, it is certainly not too much to say that Luke is a historian in whom we can confidently trust.

LUKE'S ACCURACY CONVINCES CRITIC

Any discussion of the historicity of Acts will inevitably mention the pioneer work of Sir William Ramsay. Destined to become an eminent authority on the geography and history of Asia Minor, when he first began his work on the field he was fully convinced of the critical position on the authorship of Acts. It was with some reluctance that he turned to Acts —"a highly imaginative and carefully colored account of primitive Christianity"—for possible data on the geography of Asia Minor. The evidence that he began to find, however, led him before long to a complete reversal of his former views. If you wish to read his own account of the thrilling path along which his investigation took him, you will find it in his book *The Bearing of Recent Discovery on the Trustworthiness of the New Testament.* It is the story of how terribly wrong theories spun in the ivory tower can be, and of what crucial importance are the results of first-hand investigation.

The great rightabout-face began with his discovery of an inscription indicating that Luke had been absolutely correct in locating the boundary of Phrygia and Lycaonia between the cities of Iconium and Lystra. A small thing, you say. Yes, but turning points are not normally spectacular. It had been the common critical assumption that the city of Iconium lay in the province of Lycaonia. For Luke to have said that Paul and Barnabas fled from Iconium to the cities of Lycaonia (Acts 14:6) would be like saying that a man drove his car from Chicago to Illinois. But the inscription proved that Luke was right and his critics were wrong. At that period of history Iconium *did* belong to Phrygia and Luke was perfectly correct in what he implied. This seemingly unimportant discovery on the part of Ramsay was but the first which in time led him to hold Luke to be one of the greatest of the Greek historians.

The confirmation of the Biblical record is always more striking when it occurs at a point where the critical scholars are unanimously agreed that the Bible is in error. One such place is Luke 2:1-3. Here, we are told, is some of the worst bungling to be found in the New Testament. The existence of any Imperial enrollment is doubted; we are reminded that secular records agree that Saturninus (not Quirinius as Luke states) was governor of Syria at this time; and that the whole idea of a census which would force people to return to their ancestral home was probably invented in order to accommodate Micah's prophecy that the Messiah would come from Bethlehem.

What has archaeology to say to these claims? In the first place, that such enrollments did take place is clearly illustrated by an edict of the governor of Egypt dated A.D. 104 and dug up from the sands of Egypt. It reads in part: "The enrollment by household being at hand, it is necessary to notify all who for any cause soever are outside their own administrative district that they return at once to their homes in order to carry out the customary procedure of enrollment. . . ." (cf. A. Deissmann, *Light From the Ancient East*, p. 271). These enrollments were for the purpose of determining the amount of tribute to be paid into the Roman treasury, and it was for this reason that Joseph and Mary were returning to Bethlehem.

By a careful study of the available documents, Ramsay established that the enrollments took place every fourteen years. However, this presented a problem. The enrollment in question must necessarily have been the one that Josephus says took place between 9 and 6 B.C. Now, Luke says that the governor of Syria at this time was Quirinius (Luke 2:2 ASV), but secular records show that Quirinius did not become governor until A.D. 6 and that Saturninus was governor during the time in question.[4]

Did Luke make a mistake and confuse the two governors? Hardly. Once again archaeology has vindicated the accuracy of historical detail with which Luke tells his story. An inscription found at Tiber, and later substantiated by another from Antioch, shows that Quirinius *twice* governed as an Imperial legate. The first time was between 10 and 7 B.C. when he was commander of the Roman forces in the Homonadensian War, and as such had military jurisdiction over Syria. Thus while Saturninus was the civil governor, and therefore bore the official title of procurator, Quirinius was the military governor. It also explains why, when Quirinius became governor of Syria in A.D. 6, it is said that he was "legatus of Syria *again*."

One more example of Luke's accuracy. In Luke 3:1 we have a reference to "Lysanias" who was "tetrarch of Abilene"

[4]Most readers realize that the birth of Christ, since it preceded the death of Herod, must be dated somewhere before 4 B.C. The awkwardness is due to an unfortunate mistake in the sixth century when the dating from the founding of Rome was replaced by the B.C. and A.D. system.

in the fifteenth year of Tiberius Caesar, that is, about A.D. 27. Critics considered this as another slip of the pen on Luke's part because the only ruler by that name whom the historians knew to have ruled in those parts was a Lysanias who was put to death by Mark Anthony some sixty years before (in 36 B.C.). However, we now have an inscription from Abila (near Damascus) which speaks of "Lysanias the tetrarch." Because of the particular joint title (the "Lords Imperial"—given only to Tiberius and his mother Livia) used in this inscription, it must necessarily be dated between A.D. 14 and 29, the very time indicated by Luke.

The evidence could be multiplied almost without end, but enough has been cited to show that whether the question is approached from the standpoint of historical probability and internal consistency, or from the external verification which archaeology provides, to think of Luke as anything but an accurate and trustworthy historian of primitive Christianity is to fly in the face of all probability.

### Further Archaeological Evidence

Thus far we have talked about those places where Luke is said to have been in error. We have demonstrated how archaeology has confirmed the historicity of Luke's account. Note that it is always the *historical record* which can be said to be confirmed by archaeology and not the essential truthfulness of the Christian faith itself. This assurance is inseparably involved with the response of faith and does not move in the realm of external verification. But even on the level of historical evidence, the major function of archaeology is not so much to confirm as it is to illustrate. We now turn to a number of examples where the discoveries of archaeology have thrown new light on the historical background of Christianity.

Paul's last visit to Jerusalem ended in a riot which landed him in jail. It was instigated by some Asian Jews who claimed that Paul had defiled the holy place by bringing Greeks into the temple. Gentiles were allowed to enter the outer court, but were forbidden on penalty of death to set foot in the court of the Jews. Josephus, the Jewish historian at the court of Rome, indicates that the Imperial authorities were so sensitive about not interfering in the religious practices of Judaism that they sanctioned the execution of even a Roman citizen for such an offense (*Jewish War* vi.2.4.). Between the two courts there was a lone stone barrier, about five feet in height, with notices written in Greek and Latin attached at intervals to remind the forgetful Gentile that to pass beyond that point was tantamount to suicide. In 1871, while excavating the temple site Clermont-Ganneau, the famous French orientalist, discovered a pillar with an inscription engraved in capital letters:

> *No man of another nation is to enter within the fence and enclosure round the temple, and whoever is caught will have himself to blame that his death ensues.*

Another such inscription was found in 1935.

This temple barrier was undoubtedly the source of Paul's metaphor in Ephesians 2:14 where he speaks of the "middle wall of partition" which in former times had separated Jew and Gentile but now in Christ has been broken down (a daring statement in that the actual barrier was still intact at the time Paul was writing).

At the close of his letter to the church at Rome, Paul sends the greeting of several of his Christian brethren with him at Corinth. Among them he mentions Erastus, the city treasurer (Rom. 16:23 ASV). During excavations at Corinth in 1929 a first century pavement was unearthed with the inscription, "Erastus, procurator for public building, laid this pavement at his own expense." It is quite possible that the

Erastus of the inscription and Paul's friend were one and the same person.

Acts 14 relates that Paul, after reaching Lystra on his first missionary journey, healed a man who had been crippled from birth (verses 8-10). The reaction of the crowd was to assume that the gods had come down to them in human form. They promptly designated Barnabas as Zeus, and Paul, since he was the chief speaker, as Hermes. (The King James Version uses the Roman names Jupiter and Mercury.) The people prepared to offer sacrifice to them. That these two gods were traditionally connected with this particular region is indicated by the Roman poet Ovid, who tells of a time when Zeus and Hermes came there incognito and found hospitality with a certain aged and kindly couple.

Archaeology tells the same story about the religion of that part of Asia Minor. In 1910 near Lystra an inscription was found that records the dedication to Zeus of a statue of Hermes. A few years later a stone altar was discovered which was dedicated to the "Hearer of Prayer" (Zeus?) and Hermes. These authentic reconstructions of local customs and atmosphere are significant testimonies to the ability of Luke as a careful and sensitive historian.

The site of the ancient city of Ephesus on the west coast of Asia Minor has yielded remarkable results for New Testament archaeology. On the last day in December, 1869, J. T. Wood, digging through some twenty feet of silt, came upon the pure white marble pavement of the famous temple of Artemis (Diana). This magnificent octagonal structure (referred to in Acts 19:27), with its sculptured columns and blocks of colored marble which were joined by gold rather than mortar, was truly one of the "seven wonders of the world."[5]

[5]The thrilling account of Wood's eleven years of excavations at Ephesus can be read in his *Discoveries at Ephesus*, 1877.

A few years later a group of Austrian archaeologists cleared and gave careful study to the enormous open-air theater where the riot caused by Demetrius, described in Acts 19:23-41, took place. This theater was the regular meeting place of the *ecclesia*, or civic assembly, as implied by Paul in Acts 19:32, 39, 41 (ASV) and verified by an inscription found in the theater. Adjacent to this huge structure which seated some 25,000 people were some buildings used for educational purposes. One of them may have been the hall of Tyrannus in which Paul taught the Ephesian converts for a period of two years (Acts 19:9).

Many examples of "Books of Magic," like those which the Ephesian Christians burned in public (Acts 19:19), have survived. The most famous is the Great Magical Papyrus, now in Paris, which contains such gibberish incantations as "Mimipsothiooph, Persothi, A, E, I, O, U, come out of him!" Another inscription engraved on a block of marble reads, "If the bird is flying from right to left, then whether it rises or settles out of sight, it is unlucky." It is almost impossible to realize the wealth of archaeological material unearthed at Ephesus unless one reads for himself the firsthand accounts.

Considerable light has been thrown on the history of New Testament days by the record of ancient coins. For instance, coins of Damascus have been found with the names of the Roman emperors who ruled both before and after the period of A.D. 37-54. However, none have yet been found bearing the insignia of Caligula or Claudius who were in power during this time. In II Corinthians 11:32 Paul refers to the governor under King Aretas who guarded Damascus, thus forcing him to escape over the wall. Aramaic inscriptions show that Aretas IV ruled the Nabataean Arabs from 9 B.C. until A.D. 40 and that somewhere during this time was in power at Damascus. The lack of any coin indicating Imperial rule at this juncture and the discovery of a Damascus coin with a date equivalent to A.D. 37 and bearing the image of Aretas, is an interesting confirmation of Paul's narrative.

If space permitted we could continue to set forth the amazing contribution of archaeology to an understanding of the New Testament. We have by no means exhausted the evidence. Of equal interest would be the account of the discovery of the Nazareth Stone which sheds light on the circumstances of the resurrection; the Delphi inscription which names Gallio as proconsul of Achaia in 52, and thereby provides a fixed date in Pauline chronology (cf. Acts 18:12); the two ossuaries (receptacles for bones) found in a burial chamber in use before A.D. 50 and bearing references to Jesus scratched in charcoal, and many more.

One final word should be said about the two great manuscript discoveries of the 1940's—the Coptic Gospel of Thomas and the Dead Sea Scrolls. The Gospel of Thomas, lost for sixteen centuries and discovered in 1945 in an Egyptian tomb, has been called "one of the greatest sensations of modern archaeology." It is but one of the forty-nine works which made up the thirteen bound volumes discovered at Nag Hamadi. This collection of 114 "sayings of Jesus" as recorded by "Didymus Judas Thomas" is a fourth or fifth century adaption of a work whose primitive text was produced in Greek and whose underlying sources ultimately go back to an early Jewish-Christian tradition which was parallel to but independent of the sources for our canonical Gospels. From the standpoint of textual importance, it witnesses to the fact that behind the Gospel tradition there stands a Person whose words have come down to us with no appreciable alteration. Along with the other works it provides a primary source for the complex and heretical religious movement known as Gnosticism.

The Dead Sea materials have by now become legendary. Almost every schoolboy knows the story of the Bedouin who in 1947 chanced upon the cave near Wadi Qumran which, along with others, has yielded such priceless treasures. The shepherd had been searching on a steep rock hillside for a goat that had strayed, when he came upon an opening in the rocks. Throwing a stone through the opening he heard something break. A bit apprehensive he left and returned later with a friend and the two of them, made brave by each other's presence, wiggled through the hole. Once inside the cave they saw in the dim light a number of earthen jars, some broken and others intact. Disappointed to find nothing in the jars but some old leather rolls, they set off to Bethlehem in the hope of finding someone who would be interested enough to buy them. Little did they realize that their find was of greater importance for the world than if the jars had been filled with gold.

What they had stumbled into was the literary remains of an Essene community which had had its headquarters in that area from about 150 B.C. until shortly before the fall of Jerusalem in A.D. 70. From this cave, and the others which were subsequently located in the same area, a library of more than 400 volumes has been identified. This includes manuscripts of all or part of every Old Testament book with the exception of Esther.

While the total impact of this great discovery on the study of the New Testament has not as yet been fully realized, already it has shed a great deal of new light upon the origins of Christianity and the context in which it arose. Contrary to some early and ill-advised statements to the effect that in the Qumran "Teacher of Righteousness" we have an extraordinary prototype of the Galilean Master of Christianity, the Dead Sea Scrolls have showed us more clearly the distinctive nature of Christianity over against that phase of contemporary Judaism represented in the Scrolls.

Our conclusion can be simply stated. Whether the problem of the accuracy of the New Testament is approached from the more philosophical standpoint of historical probability and inner consistency, or whether the abundant evidence of archaeology is examined with care, the Christian can rest secure in the confidence that in the New Testament he has an accurate account of God's mighty intervention into history in the person of His Son Christ Jesus to redeem for Himself a people of His own.